PACIFIC LANE

Pacific Lane

A CALIFORNIA BOYHOOD

Russell LeRoy Swigart

FITHIAN PRESS

Santa Barbara, 1996

Published by Fithian Press
A division of Daniel and Daniel, Publishers, Inc.
Post Office Box 1525
Santa Barbara, CA 93102

Book Design by Eric Larson

LIBRARY OF CONGRESS CATALOGING-IN-PUBLICATION DATA
Swigart, Russell Leroy, date
  Pacific Lane / Russell LeRoy Swigart.
    p. cm.
  ISBN 1-56474-181-8 (pbk. : alk. paper)
  1. Torrance (Calif.)—Biography. 2. Swigart, Russell LeRoy, date—Childhood
and youth. 3. Torrance (Calif.)—Social life and customs. 4. California, Southern
—Biography. I. Title.
F869.T6S95   1996
979.4'94—dc20   96-5814
                                                 CIP

FOREWORD

I am not a writer. I tell you that in advance, since I fear you might expect too much of me, and I seem unable to determine the quality of all this myself.

For years this story has oozed out of me in bits and pieces, and finally, in an attempt to just get it out of my system, I spent two serious years doing that.

When it was done, I read it and enjoyed reliving the experiences and agonized about its appeal to others.

I mustered enough courage to let some ten people read it. Eight of the ten encouraged me (thanks, Mom), and so I'll give it the old college try. If you are reading this and are about to give the rest a try, I hope it provides a chuckle or two, and more importantly, recalls a pleasant memory from your pre-teen years.

Incidentally, the events of the book are true, so essential elements like violence and overt sex are not to be found in "bestseller" quantity. Now I've done it, haven't I?

PACIFIC LANE

T he year was 1939. I was seven years old and had just learned my first lesson in standing my ground against what I perceived as overwhelming odds.

Ronnie Kronk, red-headed and possessed of a fiery, explosive, and unpredictable temper, had chased me home three times this week. My father had warned me that I only encouraged and exacerbated the problem by running. I would have to face his rage and deal with it sooner or later. He seemed convincing, but Ronnie's temper was a load.

If you knew my father, you would know I was receiving more than just advice—this was really an order! This was not a man who could condone "sissy" behavior, especially from *his* only son, and sooner or later really meant "now"!

So it was that when the next Kronk explosion came, my father's "suggestion" was forgotten and the conditioned reflex took over once again. I was headed home at flank speed, the "red peril" only a few feet behind and gaining. As the sanctity of my house appeared, my father stood on the porch and shouted, "Turn around and hit him."

What happened next will remain etched in my mind forever— which is nearly the case since this event occurred some fifty-five years ago.

At times I thought the event that occurred happened because I feared my father more than the crazy, red-headed Kronk kid, but I realize that what happened was really simply a reflex reaction; I had no reason to fear my father.

In the span of a split-second, I stopped running, turned, and stuck my fist straight at Ronnie Kronk. There was no reaction time for him—his nose impacted my fist before he could slow, dodge, or fend. I remained braced with my arm straight out where it had been at the moment of impact, hypnotized by my own unexpected action.

9

Ronnie's eyes were some double in size and filling with tears. More importantly, he was about to discover blood. When he did, he began to scream, and in another nanosecond, which seemed more like an eternity to me, he spun around and took off for *his* house.

In my amazement, I turned and looked at my father, fist still aiming at the retreating Ronnie Kronk. He issued his next order: "Chase him home!" No reason not to believe in his tactics now; I took off after my rousted enemy, fist still aimed, yelling threats and hoping fervently that he would not gain his composure and turn to face me. He did not. It was over—for all time—and my lesson was learned. Face your problems early on and head on, and life will be easier in the long run.

The Kronk incident is one of only a few memories I have of my birthplace, Chadron, Nebraska. I remember it was a very cold and windy place and that my mother hated living there, convinced the bitter cold of northwest Nebraska would shorten her life—a life hardly worth living in such a God-forsaken spot anyway, according to her.

Rescue arrived for my mother in a most unexpected way. Initially, she was humiliated by the course of events, but in retrospect, a moment of humiliation in payment for a new and wondrous life—a bargain, as she would soon admit.

❊

Things were improving economically in the early months of 1939, but the Depression was not really over for most people. Its devastating effects were everywhere: People were tired, jobs called for hard work and low pay, and one felt grateful for almost any kind of a job. A paycheck was a cherished thing.

My father worked at a flour mill, filling and stacking one hundred-pound sacks of flour eight hours a day. Hard work, but he was strong as an ox. If he felt sorry for himself working so hard for such a meager wage, I was never aware of it. He was a physical man, and the work suited him.

My father's great strength was coupled with a quick temper and fast fists—a very dangerous combination, a combination certain to cause trouble eventually—more likely sooner than later, when times are hard.

In his defense, the event I am about to relate must ultimately have had the right effect on him, because in my memory it was the last time he settled an argument in such a fashion. Another such incident probably would have exhausted my mother's patience, and he didn't want that!

They were something of an odd couple, my mother and dad—sometimes I thought their only common interest had been dancing. They courted during the heyday of touring big bands and were very compatible on the dance floor.

But marriage, the Depression and a child (me) took the dancing out of their lives, and major differences in their personalities conspired to erode their compatibility as life companions. Nevertheless, midwestern ethics dictated that people once married, stayed married—especially if children were involved. So they did, and for the most part, they made the best out of a less-than-ideal match. I was what they had in common now.

Never would my parents' differences be illustrated as overtly as one fateful day in June when my dad punched a fellow worker for reasons I was never to know. The reasons were unimportant. My mother, socially aware and dignified, was as smooth around the edges as my dad was rough. To lose one's temper was to lose one's dignity. Inexcusable. Complicating this already abhorrent form of behavior in my mother's view was the fact that the felled colleague was the husband of our neighbor and her best friend. She was mortified!

And where was I when Louie arrived home with a badly swollen and discolored eye? Where else but in his house at play with his two sons, Billy and Harold. Needless to say, I was unceremoniously dispatched to my own home. I was totally confused, since I had always been made to feel most welcome by the Deirsons, and to be chased away so rudely had me wide-eyed and frightened.

Louie's arrival had preceded my father's, so my mother at this point was as mystified as I and set out to learn from Mina (Mrs. Deirson) what I had done to deserve my expulsion. I assured her I had done nothing that would justify such treatment. The concern in her expression is still fresh in my mind; it was, I now realize, beyond what I would have seen had she thought I was somehow to blame—quarreling with the Deirson boys or being rowdy. Had she been thinking along these lines, I would not have this same image of her puzzled and pained countenance. She somehow knew something major had transpired (woman's or mother's intuition?).

My mother was right, as she soon discovered. Mina came to the door and in tears told my mother Louie's side of the story, the conclusion of which meant the termination of their friendship and the reason for Mina's tears. Friends were all that made Chadron bearable; my mother felt utterly defeated.

Strangely, I don't recall much about my father's reception when he got home, but it wasn't long before my mother's nature changed for the better—we were moving to California. The punch had cost my father his job. There was nothing holding us to Chadron any longer; we were liberated!

Just where and what California was constituted a real mystery to me at seven years of age, so my mother began the job of assuaging my anxieties with some education about the journey on which we were about to embark and the kind of place we would soon call home. It all sounded quite wonderful and exciting to me. No snow? Hard to believe. If my parents had fears, they were never in evidence when I was around. We were moving from Chadron, Nebraska to Torrance, California. It was a done deal from the start. The process had begun at the flour mill that morning, and by late afternoon we were all committed to a journey halfway across a continent, to an ocean! How amazing it all seems now.

I'm always so amazed when I see pictures of people who have left their homes and sailed into the unknown with no money, no job waiting for them, no place to live, no friends. Where do they find such courage?

At seven years old I felt no anxiety at all. It simply sounded like a grand adventure to me, and I was right. But what about my parents? Were they terrified? If not, why not? I have questioned my mother at length about her feelings at the time, and she cannot recall being frightened or especially apprehensive at all. She expresses surprise about it, too. I guess timing is everything.

My parents sold virtually everything they owned, which was not much. A couple years earlier they could not have expected to sell anything, but as I mentioned, times were improving, and people had the capability to bargain hunt.

Most of the money went to buy a 1934 Ford coupe—a very small car with only one seat, which was to transport three people and a dog (my rat terrier, Tus) from Nebraska to California. We would not know until many years later how fortunate their choice of automobile was. The little '34 Ford would become one of the most popular of all collector cars in years to come—a case of style and function coming together to produce a great car. I straddled the gearshift all the way, and Tus lay in the space between the back of the seat and the rear window, panting almost constantly. Everyone was excited, and I can still feel that excitement today.

There wasn't much about Chadron to miss. Ronnie Kronk had ceased to be a threat, but it was an uneasy truce as far as I was concerned, and the Deirson boys were nonexistent as any companion potential. As it turned out, it was good that I lost no sleep over that issue because unknowingly I was headed for "Kid City" (California), USA.

The little Ford performed as well as my father had hoped. He "worried" it across the Great Salt Desert because there were tire treads everywhere, and he didn't want ours to contribute to the litter. It was a hot, slow trip, and the least interesting portion of the journey from the standpoint of topography, but we made it without incident. Tus might have disagreed; it was hot, and she panted most of the afternoon hours. Cars were not air conditioned in 1939.

The experience that lay ahead, the Sierra, left me speechless— my most vivid recollection of the trip. The mountains were so majestic and seemed to radiate power, a blend of beauty and strength that all three of us felt. It was inspiring, and we mostly absorbed it in silence. Occasionally we would gasp in unison—mid-westerners have no concept of the existence of anything like the Sierra. My imaginings of the adventure the trip would provide were realized as we climbed and descended. A beautiful buck stood at the edge of the road as we came around a bend; we all saw it. It would have been terrible if only I had seen it. We all had the same feeling at that moment; it was a sign, and we knew we were doing the right thing, leaving Chadron.

We arrived at our destination, Torrance, California, on the

Fourth of July, Independence Day, 1939.

Things were much different in respect to this grand holiday in 1939, most notably there were firecrackers! The noise was mind boggling, and Tus was terrified, but people were having a great time with all kinds of fireworks, all illegal now—a holiday stolen by the "grinchy" fire department. A real pity in my opinion.

From the moment I learned we were moving to California, I had been consumed with the vision of "The Ocean." More correctly, I found I could not conjure up a vision of it; the idea of anything so vast was beyond me. I just couldn't wait to see it and must have asked my parents a million times just precisely when I could expect to see it. They were vague, since they really didn't know what the plans were once we arrived, or exactly how close the ocean would be. Besides, they had never seen an ocean either.

Now I have to be honest and admit that I misled you just a bit regarding our journey into the unknown. The fact is that my mother's youngest brother, my Uncle Hack, and family lived in Torrance. They had a newborn son, Gary, and Hack had a job with the A&P. That, however, was it! Their place represented bed and groceries for a few days, but nothing else. My parents knew they could not expect to extend our stay beyond a week or so, and the A&P was not hiring! My dad was in for some vigorous job hunting while my mother searched for a place to live. The Swigarts needed to get lucky.

I only perceive their problems in retrospect, since at the ripe old age of seven, I simply had some serious exploring ahead of me. I just hoped I could find some kids to play with.

We arrived at my uncle's house late that night, and even though the trip was adventurous, three long days packed into that tiny car had worn thin. I was one seven-year-old who knew how to shift through the gears. An automatic transmission would have saved my knees from a lot of bruises, but that convenience was still years away.

Poor Tus was ready to settle down, too. She had never been so confined for so long, but she was a gamer and suffered in silence, as if she realized the team, of which she was a loyal member, had to work together during this strange, confusing time. It was nearly midnight when we arrived, so I figured it was unlikely we would see the ocean before I went to bed, but I had it in mind to ask. The adults were too excited, I realized, to even suggest a trip to the beach—it would have to wait.

⛓

Let me tell you what I know about miracles.

First of all, I'm convinced that they are much more common than most people suspect, but most are viewable mainly in retrospect, rarely at the moment of occurrence. There are no bells, no colorful displays, no harp music. They happen for the most part subtly—so much so that they are unnoticed at the time. Not until later—sometimes minutes, but more usually years—do we discover that indeed, a miracle occurred. Odd coincidences, for instance, are probably more correctly minor miracles. Most people experience many miracles in their lifetimes. They are really not all that rare, depending on the degree.

The journey-weary Swigarts were about to experience a series of miracles in rather short order—a series of lucky breaks, some would say. I know better—these were bona fide miracles.

I was too excited to sleep, but too tired to lie awake, so I slept little that first night and awoke early the next morning in California. A faraway place was now here, and I was in it.

My uncle told me over toast that I would not find a scarcity of kids to play with. The neighborhood, he said, was loaded with kids of all ages. I finished my corn flakes and set out through the back door of the house to find out for myself.

The house had a large front yard but no back yard. Its rear door deposited one into an alleyway, which provided access to the tiny garage. (People did not have more than one car in 1939; they didn't have more than one bathroom, either.) Angling off the alley in front of the garage was a very narrow street, one moderate block long. The street was tiny, but the houses that lined both sides were even more diminutive. I felt a bit like Gulliver; I had never seen such little houses, not even in Chadron, and they were all identical: white, wood frame, tongue-and-groove siding. They were rectangular, but the sides varied so little, they looked square. There were seven on each side of the street; the street sign carried the name "Pacific Lane." This was to be *my* miracle.

Suddenly, as I stood looking at the cars parked with two wheels on the sidewalk so as to provide enough room for an automobile to pass by (and it was still a tight squeeze), the door of the house nearest where I stood burst open, and a barefoot, shirtless boy of approximately my age exited in full flight. Before the screen door spring could return the door to its closed position, a girl, also approximately my age, appeared in the doorway, raised an air rifle (known in my neighborhood as a "BB gun"), and calmly sighted in on the fleeing Huckleberrian-appearing boy.

To my astonishment, she pulled the trigger, sending a pellet at a rate faster than the boy could run, and when it reached its target, the ensuing death scene would have qualified for an academy award. At least *I* was convinced. The victim screamed, performed an impressive pirouette, and collapsed in the dirt just beyond the asphalt.

The girl in the doorway was given to no particular emotion at all, as far as I could see. She apparently didn't care if he was dead or not. She took in the scene of the inert body lying partway off the alleyway into the vacant lot bordering my uncle's house. One might have guessed she had just exterminated a cockroach. After a brief moment, she closed the door and disappeared into the tiny house, apparently satisfied with her marksmanship.

A few more moments passed, and as I stared, my mouth agape, I'm sure, the dead body sat up, pulled itself erect, and nonchalantly dusted itself off—not very much, only a bit—and looked my way. He didn't look happy, especially, but he obviously was not in crisis or dead, as I had feared, due to his fantastic performance. The character who had been so cruelly cut down at such a tender age was headed my way, apparently in good health.

The closer he got, the more Twainian he appeared: cut-off, faded, dirty jeans, dirty face, blond strawlike hair growing outward in all directions. His eyes were as blue as the smogless 1939 California sky, and there was an unmistakable impish sparkle to his eye. I had my first friend in California, and there wouldn't be a trace of the Ronnie Kronk temperament in my new friend, Harold.

No bells, bright lights, or colorful display, but my miracle was underway—the miracle of the Pacific Lane kids and specifically Harold, a born entertainer and my ticket to many fun-filled California days.

⋈

We could never have been mistaken for one another, Harold and I.

Harold was a "California kid," sunburned, and his feet—not only were they unshod, but they were "California feet"; they looked nothing like Nebraska feet. My feet had blood vessels, lots of them. A vascular surgeon could have used my feet instead of a textbook. Blue lines in milky white skin.

Harold's feet had no veins at all. The sun and stains from exposure to everything made them veinless and tougher than Goodyear tires. My toes were stuck together, while his spread over the ground like two thick, brown fans. They seemed to grip the ground as he walked.

When I went to bed my clothes disappeared and were replaced by a new set, sterilized and in perfect condition, of course.

Harold wore the same clothes day after day. Today he looked exactly as he did yesterday; tomorrow he would be unchanged, ragged and stained.

Harold's mother, Anna, was dressed and gone to work before Harold was awake. Harold would arise and put on the same ensemble every day. His hair showed no signs of ever having been brushed or combed; the way it grew was the way it continued until the shears interrupted the process temporarily.

Harold had no anxieties—a product of having no responsibilities. The sole negative in his life was his sister, Gloria, who had a flash point only one or two degrees from normal. Harold was the living, breathing torch. Mere proximity resulted in ignition, producing a scene out of character for the entire peaceful neighborhood.

The process was a mystery to me. I liked them both and could never understand why they were constantly at war. It was just the natural state between them, and I think they both wanted it that way. Incredibly, Harold did not seem to fear Gloria, but he always retreated when Gloria blew. Flirting with death was one thing, but jumping on a live grenade was something else again.

Comic books were Harold's passion, and his collection was impressive. It was the only thing he really kept in any sort of order. He could locate a given issue with only the slimmest of clues.

"Do you remember the story where the Green Lantern fell into the molten steel?" I would ask. In moments Harold would have the issue out of his mountainous stack and opened to the episode of my reference.

Harold read each comic book many times. The first reading didn't seem to diminish his zeal for the contents when read a second, third, or fourth time. He would trade comic books and then retrieve his originals, since most kids didn't save them very long and didn't mind giving them back.

Harold's dedication to comic books did not interfere with play. He was ready for any suggestion regarding games. He made play an art form and could raise a "play posse" in minutes. He was Tom Sawyer come to life.

As you might surmise, not everybody saw Harold in such positive terms. My mother would have preferred a much neater, cleaner Harold. My dad thought, despite his great energy, that Harold was extremely lazy. To their credit, they said little about their feelings, since he was a playmate, not a role model.

But Harold did have impressive qualities. He was, as I described, a master playmate, always in a good mood, often clowning, ready with a memorized list of play options available for instant reference. He was the nucleus of my Pacific Lane existence.

☒

While I explored the kid population in and around Pacific Lane, my parents could waste no time solving the serious problems: food and shelter. Problems don't get more serious than these.

The objectives were easily defined. My father needed to find a job, a rare commodity in Torrance, and my mother needed to find us a house. Did she have money for a deposit? I can't imagine that she did, but perhaps they weren't required then.

The house next door to my uncle's was nearly close enough to touch; next to that a vacant lot and then another small house owned by a Romanian couple, the Schultzes. They owned, I would learn, all the properties just described. Mr. Schultz was retired, a big man who walked with a cane. Mrs. Schultz was slightly more than four feet tall and never had teeth to my knowledge. She was "Schultzie" to my parents, and for reasons we will never quite understand, she and Mr. Schultz took a special and immediate liking to my parents. Talk about good fortune, they just happened to be here from Europe, happened to own the properties and happened to like us. Go figure!

The Schultzes were an astonishing story out of another culture. Mr. Schultz had been married to Schultzie's mother; Schultzie was a daughter by a previous marriage. When the mother died, Mr. Schultz took his stepdaughter as his wife, and they had made it work. A story worthy of a book, told in a simple paragraph.

My mother's miracle had materialized. We moved into the house next door to my uncle; 631 Sartori Street would be our new home. Pacific Lane was right outside my back door, so her miracle only validated my miracle.

✠

Harold was unhurt by the BB in the back. He explained that Gloria apparently had a temper like Ronnie Kronk's, and reached for the air rifle whenever Harold ignited her fuse. It turned out that Harold was some months younger than I and Gloria a bit older. They just did not get along—a situation I never understood. An only child, I always thought it would be wonderful to have a brother or sister. I still think that way, but if I had used them as an example, my attitude surely would have changed.

Anyway, Harold was mainly interested in my potential as a comic-book-swapping friend; Harold was obsessed with comic books. He was disappointed to learn that I had none, but then realized that his collection gave him great status. I was soon to become a comic book addict as well, thanks to Harold, who introduced me to the superheros of the day: Superman and Captain Marvel ruled supreme, Batman a distant third.

I was not as comfortable as Harold was with someone I had just met. It was as though he had known me forever. Was it because he was on home turf? No. As I was to learn, this was just Harold: uninhibited, energetic, friendly, and good natured.

Harold soon revealed to me the miracle of Pacific Lane. Incredibly, almost all of the little Pacific Lane houses contained kids—kids our age, kids we would play with and grow up with. There were more kids on Pacific Lane than in the whole town of Chadron, it seemed. A key point was that except for a couple of girls, I was the oldest, just slightly, but nonetheless, the oldest kid in the neighborhood. Instant status was mine, but Harold's effervescence and entertaining nature would be a serious challenge to my "King of the Hill" position.

✸

My father's job hunting was not going well. There were no flour mills in or around Torrance. In fact, there was precious little of anything. The town was encircled with small farms providing only seasonal crop harvesting, and industry was represented by only two major companies: a steel mill (Columbia Steel, a division of U.S. Steel) and an oil well machinery and tool company (National Supply). These two firms supplied jobs to a great majority of the working-class people of the town and surrounding area. The problem was, my father did not have skills appropriate to these companies' needs, but more importantly, they were not hiring anyway.

Mr. Schultz was getting on my father's nerves. Living next door as he did, he was monitoring my father's agonizingly unsuccessful attempts to find employment; being asked about it every day was wearing thin.

Mr. Schultz had retired from Columbia Steel, having reached sixty-five years of age. How old was he now? I had no idea, but I thought he was ancient! He sure was not feeble or senile, though, an imposing, slightly gruff old man who was nice enough to me but who I minded my manners around. I was intimidated, but I liked him. I loved Shultzie, and the feeling was mutual. We were great pals.

One day, after a long, frustrating day of job hunting, my father was unable to avoid Mr. Schultz. My father had a jaunty walk. Anyone who knew him well could recognize him from a distance because of his distinctive step, but the bounce was beginning to disappear along with his unemployment benefits and any prospect of employment. Things were getting a bit desperate.

Mr. Schultz intercepted my dad, and rather than inquire as to my father's success (or lack of it) that day, he asked my father for a moment of his time. My father's spirits sank further, since he felt that the usual short inquiry was about to stretch into a proportionately unpleasant long inquiry. He didn't need this. Instead, my father found himself being advised that he was going about the whole job hunting challenge in the wrong fashion. Not welcome news; my father was not good at taking criticism. But Mr. Schultz was not one to be intimidated by a disapproving expression. He plowed ahead and in so doing, my dad's miracle was in the making.

Fortunately for us all, my father paid close attention to Mr. Schultz's instructions (not advice), and the next day my father set out feeling that while he did not have a job, at least he had a tactic—a plan. A bit of the bounce returned to his step. Mr. Schultz's directions had made a major impression on him. At 8:00 a.m. my father was waiting for the employment door to open at Columbia Steel. He had been there many times and had always received the "Sorry, no hiring today" response, after which he would depart for his next stop at National Supply Company, and a similar scene would ensue. Today, however, was different.

My father simply walked over to one of the two or three wooden chairs across from the desk and sat down, following the usual rejection. As minutes ticked by, he began to receive quizzical looks from the office staff. He made eye contact with them and continued to sit where he was.

After some twenty or thirty minutes, my dad was asked if there was something else. He expressed his thanks and advised the inquirer that he would wait in case anything came up. The inquirer expressed the opinion that she did not think it likely that there would be an opening that day, but my father remained seated and indicated he had nothing better to do—no better prospects than to hope something opened up for him here at Columbia Steel—"the company he most wanted to work for." The inquirer went back to her duties.

Noon arrived, and my father opened his lunch sack and ate his lunch, being careful to make no mess that would aggravate anyone. He could sense the discomfort of the staff, but ignored their nervousness and continued to make eye contact with anyone who looked his way.

At 5:00 p.m. he gathered himself and his lunch sack, announced courteously that he would return tomorrow, and left. It had been a long, emotionally draining day, but my father felt just that tiniest bit more successful as he walked the half mile to our house, his mill cap at a rakish angle. He was again recognizable from a distance.

As he promised, he returned the next day, and after the usual question and routine response, he again took up station on the same chair as on the previous day. He was aware of eyeballs rolling up and nervous glances between members of the office staff, but he gave no indication that he noticed. He was, of course, much more uncomfortable than he allowed them to know, but Mr. Schultz had told my father he would get a job if he did not give up. He was not going to give up!

On the fifth day, one of the office staff said to a supervisor passing through, "Will you *please* give that guy" (pointing to my dad) "a job? We're sick of looking at him and he is not going to go away." In the next moments, my father became an employee of Columbia Steel, where he worked as a millwright for the next twenty-five years. My dad's miracle had materialized.

Mr. Schultz would get on my dad's nerves many times over the years, but his gratitude outweighed his aggravation. The Schultzes had supplied two miracles, and we would be in their debt forever—an IOU that would never be called.

Harold set about to introduce me to Pacific Lane's juvenile society. A childless family named Shepherd lived next to Harold and Gloria, and in the next house lived Harold's best friend, Albert (Boo) Knappenberger, an older sister, Daisy, and a younger brother, Richard (never called Dick). In that tiny house, a family of five!

We walked up to Albert's house. Harold took a deep breath and demonstrated the method used to summon one of the neighborhood kids. You didn't knock or ring the doorbell (was there a doorbell?); you just called out his or her name at the top of your lungs. In this case, "BOO-Oooo." A moment's wait and then repeat, "BOO-Oooo."

That did it! The door opened and another barefoot preadolescent kid stood in the doorway. Harold suggested he "come on out and play," and I met my second friend, Boo. My social life in California was off and running.

Boo's tiny house provided shelter for five people, and all three kids grew up there, which at the time did not seem extraordinary. Now I can't imagine how it was accomplished. The houses could not have been more than 400 or 500 square feet, with one bedroom, one bathroom, and a fold-down Murphy bed in the living room. Amazingly, as time passed, the house became the meeting place for kids of all ages: Daisy's older girlfriends, Boo's friends, and Richard's younger friends. Everyone was welcome there. Mr. and Mrs. Knappenberger were both known as "Knappy," and they were just wonderful. Originally from Pennsylvania, Father Knappy was a deer hunter and had a number of rifles. They were of great interest to us boys, of course, especially the lever-action Winchester .30-.30. What a beauty!

Mr. Knappenberger worked at Columbia Steel, too, and would talk about no car other than the "Nash Ambassador." It was the only point of major disagreement I had with him that I can recall. I thought Nashes were awful cars.

Mother Knappy's Christmas trees belonged in Macy's window. People came from all over town to see them, and I even took my future wife to see one long after I moved from the neighborhood. They were spectacular, adorned with unique ornaments most of us had never seen before, and an entire town at the base complete with an electric train, waterfall, and pond. You had to be there to really appreciate the grand display. Did anyone mind that now there was no room to even turn around? Not in the least. The spectacle was obviously worth the inconvenience.

Our summer days were spent playing and reading. We alternated between "cops and robbers," comic books, kick the can, comic books, hide and seek, comic books, and "vacant lot." Our big vacant lot represented a game all its own, an informal theme park.

Out in the center grew a huge iceplant. It was our "creeping monster." We hacked away at it with wooden swords, but nothing could keep it from moving ever closer to our cave, our "safe place." The cave was a hole we had dug and placed boards over. We then covered the boards with dirt. A great deal of growing up took place in that cave as we exchanged bits and pieces of developmental information—some valid, some not so valid. Often we became more confused than enlightened, but trial and error is more effective than we often want to admit, and as we moved puzzle pieces around, sooner or later they formed a fairly accurate picture.

As summer progressed, I was as happy as a kid could be, but my first day in a California school lay ahead—a situation that lurked in the recesses of my mind. At age seven there is no future, there is only now, and school was days, perhaps even weeks away. I was far too busy to worry about something so distant.

✖

After a time I became aware that Harold and Gloria lived only with their mother. There was no Mr. Chapman in evidence. This was an uncommon arrangement to me. I was able to recall only one other such situation, which involved a friend of my mother's in Chadron—my Aunt Miller. There was no comparable arrangement among the kids of Pacific Lane. Everybody had a mom and a dad.

The mother, Anna, was a tall, slim lady who stood ramrod straight, and when she set out for work in the morning (another departure from the neighborhood norm), she set a pace faster than anyone I had ever seen. She seemed serious, but that was understandable, considering the constant state of war between Harold and Gloria. There was little peace and quiet in Anna's life. She was raising two strong-willed kids by herself.

Because I was Harold's friend, Anna accepted me like I was one of her own, characteristic of parents in the neighborhood. The Knappys treated me the same way.

There was an uncommon bonus associated with Anna's attitude, however. Anna was the sole waitress at the most popular malt shop in Torrance, Howdy's, perhaps the most important business establishment in town.

Imagine what this meant! There was little extra money for fountain treats, as my parents struggled to regain some economic equilibrium, but that became inconsequential, since Harold and I were never more than a three-quarter-mile walk from a thick chocolate malt or hot fudge sundae. Adding to this bonanza was the largest supply of comic books in town, and finally, the place was always alive with older kids who envied our relationship with Anna and the owner, Howdy. Was Torrance another word for heaven, I wondered?

The Chapman father, I learned from Harold, was in the Navy and visited his family only rarely. I was not suspicious, and this news served to elevate Harold's status with me even more. He had never lied to me or exaggerated anything enough to doubt him. My hope was that his father would visit soon so I could meet a real live military person. I pictured Don Winslow of the Navy, a comic book hero.

One day it happened, but it was not the scene I had imagined. Lying on the tiny couch in the tiny living room was a handsome fellow about my uncle's age, in a white tee shirt and navy blue bell bottoms. Harold's dad was home. He was holding a piece of raw meat on his eye and gave no indication he wanted to socialize or even meet me.

As Harold and I sat on the door stoop thumbing through dog-eared comic books, Harold told me that his mother had hit his father in much the same fashion my father had struck Louie. As a result, Harold's dad, like Louie, had a serious shiner. The reason behind the fracas? Harold had no idea, and seemed to care not at all.

Further inquiry on my part indicated that the parents had a relationship much like Harold's and Gloria's. Apparently Mr. Chapman could expect less than a welcome reception from Anna on his rare visits, and perhaps he hadn't been as far out to sea as I had imagined. Avoiding home perhaps?

As much as I liked Harold's mother, I was not very impressed with the fact that she apparently had no trouble emerging victorious in these domestic set-to's. My male ego tended to reject the possibility of a woman besting a man in actual physical combat, but then Harold never waited around to challenge Gloria in a hand-to-hand, close-quarters contest either, and I didn't blame him a bit. Gloria's temper was of ballistic proportions and Harold's was nonexistent. The same was almost certainly true of the parents, but a military man beaten up by a woman? It was a puzzle to me!

⚓

When school started, I was in for some surprises in the form of browns and yellows—skins, that is. There had been no Mexican or Japanese kids in Chadron, Nebraska, but there were lots of them at Torrance Elementary. I seemed to be the only one who noticed.

Gloria Chapman and another Pacific Laner, Martha Ossea, were the only kids in my grade whom I knew. The problem with that was they knew everyone, it seemed. Actually there were other new kids too, so my entry into third grade went pretty smoothly, and I soon learned that my basic skills were ahead of my new classmates—most of them that is. Chizuko and Sakio, two little Japanese girls, were exceptions. They were really smart. They would become good friends in the next two years, before all hell broke loose.

I wasn't crazy about school academically, but it was a social Garden of Eden. I met kids that first day that I would graduate from high school with, including Gloria and Martha. We didn't lose many kids along the way, and in fact we picked up a bunch. Southern California in general, and Torrance in particular, was experiencing a long, steady population increase. California looked like the promised land to millions of people trying to scratch out a living anywhere doing anything. It was hard to find a kid who had been born in California. Harold and Gloria were exceptions.

Across the playground at Torrance Elementary were about a half-dozen wooden one-room classrooms. They were called "the bungalows." This is where the slow kids were taught, and in most cases, "slow" meant Mexican. Because of their exiled situation, many of them were defensive and hostile. The problem was they could not understand the lessons because they spoke little or no English and the teachers spoke no Spanish—a disaster in the making. We were given to believe they were dumb. Of course they were not dumb at all. They were the victims of ignorance, not the ignorant.

The problem has not gone away. It persists today, and as a result, Latinos drop out of school at a high rate and suffer the obvious and predictable results: gang activity and unemployment.

My mother was not too pleased that I got on well with them and often brought them home after school. She would insist that the ones who were my friends were not Mexican at all but "Castillian" or "high Spanish." Meaningless terms, but it made her feel better. In her defense, she never, never told me not to play with them. Many Anglo parents were not so wise in this respect. My exposure to Mexican children had a positive influence on my racial tolerance in later life, so I applaud my mother's wisdom regarding all this.

My dad, to my memory, never said a word about it, which is really odd, considering that he had little good to say about any minority. Looking back, I have attributed his bigotry to the Depression, which made everyone seem so competitive and defensive. Racial paranoia was very common to the times.

None of this attitude rubbed off on me. Why, I don't really know, but I was more fascinated by the differences in people than threatened. As a result, I had a lot more friends.

School became an extension of Pacific Lane: one set of friends during weekdays and another after school and on weekends. It just doesn't get much better than that, and I was happy.

There was, however, a new sadness in my life at this time; not all the family had experienced a miracle. My dog, Tus, did not find California such a wondrous new home at all. Apparently California fleas lie in wait for midwestern immigrant canines; they began to overwhelm her and none of the conventional control systems seemed to be effective. She was frantic and we suffered for her as all attempts to win the battle failed.

In desperation my father tried a home remedy concocted by a well-meaning friend. He rubbed the stuff on her and then left her for a moment to wash his hands. He heard her give a yelp, but when he went back to the yard, she was gone. We never saw her again. We searched and put up notices, to no avail. My loyal, loving companion, Tus, was gone forever, leaving a terrible void felt by the whole family.

Having a pet is a great experience, but losing one is an early lesson in what emotional commitment is all about. The void created by the absent, adoring, dependent friend overwhelmed me. I had experienced an example of how dangerous it is to take such fragile relationships for granted, and how painful the loss of a loved and loving friend can be, but also how rewarding and fulfilling a relationship of significant commitment is. Agonizingly bittersweet, the threat of heartbreak is always lurking in the shadows.

IX

Music was a big part of kid life then, as it is now. The radio was the family entertainment center and much of the air time was devoted to music and those who made it.

A major difference was the fact that kid music and adult music were the same music. Today a chasm separates the two, and it seems to widen continually.

Can we say the names were bigger then? Hard to say, but they were certainly more enduring, generally speaking.

Bing Crosby was the "main man," by a wide margin. He dominated radio with Kraft Music Hall, he dominated the recording business on the Decca label, and he dominated films with his "Road" pictures, which also featured the dominant comedian, Bob Hope. Crosby could do it all. It was said he was the most recognizable person in the world.

There was plenty of room for others: Perry Como, Billy Eckstein, Frankie Laine, the Ink Spots, the Mills Brothers, King Cole Trio, and Tony Martin, just to name a few.

The ladies were represented by Judy Garland, Ginny Simms, Helen O'Connell, Jeanette McDonald, Wee Bonnie Baker, Deanna Durbin, and others.

It was also the heyday of the big bands: Miller, Dorsey, James, Martin, Brown, Lombardo, and Kenton. Benny Goodman, the "King of Swing," did magic things on his clarinet. These names remained popular for years—decades even—not just weeks or months.

I don't mean to imply the music was all that superior. We had some classics that have not endured. "Mares-E-Doats," "Hutsut Ralson on the Ritherah," "Hot Diggity Dog Ziggity Boom," "Three Little Fishies"—these were huge hits and nearly moronic in content. Spike Jones and Ish Kabibble were comic musicians.

The kid–adult polarization arrived in the form of a skinny, almost anorexic-appearing, bow-tied guy who looked like a skeleton with hair. Girls started "swooning" and became known as "bobby soxers." They went crazy for this guy.

We boys and the adults were puzzled. The voice was good enough, but what was the great attraction? He was so "geeky" looking.

Frankie was about to teach us what "charisma" was all about. He would ultimately capture us all...forever. But kids discovered that music could distance them from the controlling adult world, and as parents accepted Sinatra, kids began to look elsewhere. Frankie started it all. He created the seam that would become the chasm.

I really liked music. I had a pleasant voice and could sing any popular song. I knew the lyrics to all of them, and I went around singing most of the time. Unlike those precocious kids who "perform," however, I simply sang for my own enjoyment. I always wished I had some talent to display my talent, but alas, I did not. What little there was, was wasted. I had no ham in me.

My mother recognized the potential and tried on more than one occasion to expose the song-and-dance man she thought might be trying to come out. I would take lots of music lessons: singing, dancing and clarinet. It wasn't so much that I didn't want to do those things as it was a distraction from my time with my kid friends. Practice was a solitary exercise, and I had no patience with solitude.

I would stick to the clarinet because I liked the idea of playing in a band—right in character—turning everything into a social event. But dancing was "sissy stuff," and I had a reputation among the kids to protect. Also mitigating against a career in the performing arts was a growing awareness that I was pretty good at sports. Now we were on to something!

Gradually the vacant lot became a sports arena, featuring touch football games and "work-up." Playing cops and robbers and Superman games was giving way to playing catch with a baseball and practicing passing the football. I was nine, and I had a most adventurous year ahead. We're talking about 1941—an eventful and fateful year for everyone—everyone in the entire world.

✖

What I wanted more than anything in the world was a bike. It seemed to me that all the kids my age had bikes. Not true, but it seemed like it to me.

My dad had his own ideas about this bike business, namely that the proper age to own a bike was ten years old *minimum*! His second condition was that a person desiring such a major possession be required to contribute in a major way to its purchase price. This meant I was going to be required to make some adjustments in my social life and convert my recreational activities to some form of money-generating activity. At nine, such conflicts are tough to resolve.

I decided to go for the bike. After all, my social life at school would remain intact; only the neighborhood activities would face curtailment.

I sought my dad's counsel on the subject of how I could earn the required money, and how much were we talking about anyway? He suggested a two-step approach: First I would need to find work and second we would research the price of bikes.

We scanned the want ads together and learned that I was too young for a paper route, and would have needed a bike anyway, but I could qualify to sell magazines door to door. So if one discounts regular chores (drying dishes, keeping room picked up, making bed), I had my first job. I was a *Saturday Evening Post* and *Ladies' Home Journal* salesman. Time to check out the bikes. I was going to make some big-time, serious money. Everybody read magazines, didn't they?

When I was nine my maternal grandmother, Ellen, came to live with us. She was Swedish and a wonderful addition to the family, especially for me. Her presence made it possible for my mother to go to work. Mom had completed a correspondence course in bookkeeping and quickly landed a job at Western Auto Supply. My grandmother was cook, housekeeper, and companion to the family. She was superb at all three.

Grandma Ellen was the most stereotypical grandmother imaginable. All my friends considered her "their" grandmother. She could have been Andy Hardy's grandmother quite easily. Grandmothers should be old, and right in character, my grandmother was old. She was always old. She never got older in my mind; she was just always old. It was not a negative thing.

Grandma Ellen had lived a hard life. My grandfather had been killed in a railroad-related accident and had left her with nothing but housekeeping skills to raise Harold, Amy, Estella, my mother, Esther, and Orville. How did she do it?

None but Orville (Hack) would finish high school. These kids, however, were not dropouts as we know them today. These were people needed to help put food on the table and a roof over their heads. Each would have done almost anything to remain in school.

But they all survived, and after years of scrubbing floors, polishing furniture, and cooking for others, Grandma Ellen was home with family—an equal. The work might be the same, but the feeling was, for her, like being reborn.

Grandmothers wore lace-up shoes reserved for old ladies. Grandma Ellen did too. She and I shared a bed for a couple of years, and in the mornings I would watch her struggle into a corset, which was worn over her underclothes. It had to be terribly uncomfortable, but she wore it every day, even though her days were very active (not at my parent's insistence, but as a result of her own motivation). Our house was spotless. She did not consider herself retired. She was, in her view, a full-time contributor to the family needs. My parents could not have hired a more motivated person.

Grandma Ellen's self-assigned duties did not, however, include any disciplinary responsibility. Our relationship was purely grandmother and grandson. We were great pals and in my memory a cross word never passed between us. I was not really unique in that respect. Grandma Ellen was very protective of any relative, and we learned to keep any criticism to ourselves lest we receive a lecture. My maternal relatives could do no wrong in her eyes, and though many were undeserving of this inordinate loyalty, we respected it. If we couldn't keep quiet, we made sure to keep her out of hearing range.

My home began to rival Howdy's in the gastronomic sense. Pies, cakes, cookies, coffee cakes, jelly rolls, cinnamon rolls. There was always some delicious dessert and usually choices. She was so pleased and grateful to be with us. I had no idea anything was missing before she came (except a bike), but she brought a whole new dimension to my life at home.

It seemed a bit out of character for my dad to be so receptive to the arrangement, but he was. His attitude impressed people, as well it should have. There were others of her children who could have picked up the slack, but rarely did. They were perfectly willing to let my parents assume the lion's share of the responsibility. Their loss and our gain, as far as I was concerned.

With my mother working and contributing a second income, the

Swigart finances were improving at a rapid pace. There was one more potential advantage of my mother's employment—"Western Flyer" bikes, perhaps at a discount! I was not getting rich on sales of *Saturday Evening Post* and *Ladies' Home Journal*, and I wanted that bike more than anything. Not everyone read magazines, I was learning.

✖

I found myself facing a crisis in school—a most unfamiliar position for me.

While I never applied myself like I was a candidate for valedictorian, still I had experienced no problem keeping up with class work, but at this moment I sat puzzled, wondering what was going on. The teacher was talking about "fractions" as if they were the most normal things in the world. To me they were entirely alien! Where had they come from? Where was my wandering mind when they were first addressed? How could 3/4 and 7/8 be compatible?

As I looked around, no one seemed confused or panicky, which only made me feel worse. As usual, Chizuko and Sakio looked eager to move on to something even more mysterious and complicated than the stuff being discussed now. That was no surprise, but it *was* a surprise when the teacher announced a test on the subject scheduled for tomorrow!

Of course all this anxiety could have been eliminated had I raised my hand and admitted I did not understand about numbers broken into pieces which could somehow be added, subtracted, multiplied, and divided, and unlike Humpty Dumpty, become all put together again. But I didn't. I was afraid of the potential humiliation which represented a slightly worse prospect than failing the test. A real "lose–lose" situation, and I did not feel prepared to handle it.

The bell rang, the school day was over and I was seated, comatose except for the tears welling up in my eyes. Ordinarily I would have led the charge through the door to freedom from classroom constraint. Perhaps seeing me still seated is what caught their eyes, but whatever it was, Chizuko and Sakio approached me and expressed their concern.

Reluctantly I admitted my fractional deficiency, and as if it were the most natural thing in the world for them to do, they sat down with me—Chizuko beside me and Sakio in front of me. Through them I entered, at the most fundamental level, the world of fractions—explained so logically a goldfish could have gotten it. The important thing was *I* got it! I was transformed from a preadolescent basket case to a mathematical genius, or so it felt at the moment.

Their kindness was an expression of sensitivity uncommon to kids our age. I was so grateful and felt so lucky that they had noticed and actually followed up as they did. They didn't give me time to withdraw into self-consciousness or embarrassment, and when it was over, Chizuko and Sakio had a lifetime admirer. I never had to stand up and fight for them, but I would have.

I passed the test easily; why wouldn't I? My volunteer tutors had prepared me so well that aside from themselves, I was more proficient at fractions than any of my classmates. Life was worth living again, thanks to my little Japanese-American lifesavers.

✖

I was more apprehensive than usual about my school work because I wanted to go to YMCA camp in the summer, and I knew that if I appeared to be lagging in school, I would be in summer school instead. Summer school carried a stigma that no one wanted, not to mention the kink it put in one's enjoyment of that great institution, summer vacation.

The fact that I had never been away from my parents had not yet occurred to me since I had fallen under the seductive spell of Harold's vivid description of camp: swimming, hiking, campfires, etc. in the beauty of the magnificent mountains like I had seen on my way to California. It sounded wonderful, and I had pestered my parents at every opportunity. Bike, camp, and dog—those were the topics my parents were bombarded with incessantly. The jury, however, was still out on all three counts, and my performance in school was a topic I didn't need to be reminded about. It was a given. No good grades, "no nothin'"! I might have been an only child, but my parents displayed a united front, and once the game rules were expressed, they were cast in bronze. No appeal possible.

Another situation of similar rigid premise was that once I took something on, I was expected to finish. No quitting! When the going got rough, or if things turned out more difficult than I expected, I had better look for a way to make it work. This business with magazine sales was a good example. Not as easy or rewarding as I had imagined, but necessary. And until I earned my required bike share, there was no way out anyway.

An additional lesson was the fact that seemingly unrelated things often had a great deal in common: the bike, school, magazine sales, camp. They were all linked together and a misstep could mess everything up. If I didn't go to camp, I probably wouldn't get a bike either—a situation too grim to contemplate.

I had some regular *Saturday Evening Post* customers and far fewer *Ladies' Home Journal* regulars. The rest of my sales required door-to-door effort. I studied this ponderous system, seeking an improved approach—a new market for the books, an easier, faster way. My inspiration came like a bolt from the blue. Why hadn't I thought of it before?

My father was a shift worker at the steel mill, and when he worked days, I often met him at the main gate and walked home with him. At 4:30 in the afternoon, a lot of workers came out of that gate, and exposing my magazines to scores of people at one time rather than trudging from door to door seemed like a most efficient approach to me.

I positioned myself at the main gate and waited for the shift whistle. Shortly after it sounded off and I saw the army of departing workers approaching, I sounded off. With as much volume as I could muster, I hawked my wares: "*Saturday Evening Post! Ladies' Home Journal!*" (No ladies worked shift work at Columbia Steel.) The surprised guard looked my way, smiled, and turned back to greet occasional workers. About every ten seconds or so, I let go with another blast as the homeward-bound workers passed by me. And now the guard was no longer smiling. Holding his ears, he gave me a scowl. I was getting on his nerves.

When I saw my dad come into view, I let go with my best. To my surprise he cringed like someone had hit him in the testicles. Before he could get to me, I let go with another good one, and that quickened his pace considerably. With his hand over my mouth, I was leaving the area at a pace too fast to call walking but just short of

•

running. Obviously the Chairman of the Board was not in favor of my marketing program.

My dad was not a man who enjoyed having attention pointed his way, and he never developed the ability to laugh at himself. This is a tragic flaw—a condition that makes moments like the one I had just produced an exaggerated embarrassment, one he should have enjoyed along with his co-workers, but instead his psyche interpreted as humiliating. Wow! Not the reaction I anticipated, but when we were safely away from his fellow workers, to his credit, he all but admitted it was really his problem and not mine.

So we walked home together, he with his hand on my shoulder while advising that the guards would probably get in trouble for permitting too much noise at the gate. It was okay. Walking home with my dad seemed better than selling magazines or even riding bikes. Kids and dads don't have enough moments like these.

I had sold a few magazines before my dad arrived on the scene, so I decided to retain the marketing approach but change the territory. Next week I would be at the main gate of the National Supply Company. I couldn't be in two places at once anyway.

The alley at my back door went all the way to Torrance Blvd. Make a right turn, two blocks and there's Howdy's. Harold and I made the trip so often I could have walked it blindfolded and described my surroundings as I went. It covered about three fourths of a mile.

What really bugged me was that Harold would always find things. I would never find anything. As we walked he would invariably say, "Look what I found." Dammit, I would think to myself, why didn't I see that first? I just never did. He would find a perfectly good pocket knife with the blade broken, maybe only the tip, a necklace with only a few beads missing, a ring with no stone, marbles with hardly a flaw—really good stuff! Sometimes he found money: nickels, dimes, or pennies. In the early '40s they were all spendable.

The candy counters of the day were full of penny candy. Most of the major candy bars of today—Hershey, Baby Ruth, Tootsie Roll, and many others—had pretty darn good-sized penny offerings. Of course, you must realize the full-size offering cost only a nickel, as did a Coca Cola, Pepsi (12 oz.), Nehi, Creme Soda, or Delaware Punch.

So, unlike today, when a penny might lie in full view of scores of people and not move for days, then it had value, and it was picked up by the first person who saw it; and it seemed to me it was always Harold who saw it first.

Perhaps it had something to do with going barefoot. Harold wore shoes only to school, as did most of the Pacific Lane kids. Me, I was a pair of feet in search of a sharp piece of glass and would find it if I walked ten feet from my back door. I knew it was drippy (a drip was a nerd or a wimp back then) to wear shoes to play in the neighborhood, but it hurt to step on glass, so I remained shod—not in sneakers, no, no, no! A kid usually only had one pair of shoes and they were of the oxford variety.

Whatever it was, I really envied Harold's built-in metal detector and thanked my stars for sports, for it became more and more evident that I was the superior athlete of the neighborhood, providing some all-important status points. Keeping ahead of Harold's talents took some doing.

So as we walked the alley to Howdy's and whatever treat Harold's mother put before us, Harold found things, and we talked about camp. In arts and crafts, I learned from Harold, I would be making a leather wallet for one of my parents. It would have his initials engraved on it. Camp sure sounded wonderful, according to Harold's description. What a grand experience I had in store!

⌘

Tus, our missing rat terrier, was a rather common breed of dog in the '30s and '40s. They fell into a category of "not pedigreed, but well-bred dogs," popular because of their size, a manageable twenty-five pounds; their appearance, alert, clean and well proportioned; and their intelligence and coordination, which made learning somewhat easier than it was for many breeds. Finally, they fit themselves into the family, another expression of their intelligence. The name "rat terrier?" No cat was a match at catching rodents. Rat terriers were in a class by themselves!

So it was no great coincidence, really, that the Schultzes had a fine female rat terrier named Sally, and so it was that these people who had already produced such a profound positive impact on us— miracles, as I have related—once again presented me with an answer to one of my big three prayers: a dog to replace my departed Tus. Sally was about to have puppies, and I was first in line, Mrs. Schultz told me, with my parents' blessing, of course.

White with brown spots, Lucky, who had a pattern on her forehead that made one think of a horseshoe, became my constant companion and the neighborhood dog from my ninth year until I was twenty-one. She loved everyone in the neighborhood and tolerated no intrusion by other dogs. Regardless of size, she dispatched them immediately upon discovery. She had no intention of sharing us or the neighborhood. Of course, she was most dedicated and loyal to our family and to me in particular. She was my dog and I was her boy. My wish list was down to two: bike and camp. How could one explain dog replacement right down to breed? Not a miracle?

✠

I had been having a bit of a problem with sore throats. For no apparent reason, my tonsils would swell up and hurt, so my mother hauled me off to the doctor for some discussion on the subject. Of course, they did all the discussing while I was kept busy with a dog-eared, ancient comic book in the reception room.

Medically speaking, the '40s were the decade of tonsillectomies. Tonsils were deemed one of God's errors. Bring a kid in with tonsils and things went on automatic. Serious decisions were underway in that doctor's office. Another mother had fallen into the hands of someone who could make her child healthier—an easy sell. All this while the victim was blissfully distracted by a poor, lame kid named Billy Batson, who could be transformed into a superhero named Captain Marvel by shouting the word "Shazam!" It could happen, I thought.

On the way home (my mother had just learned to drive and I was nervous) my mother began to soften up the victim. Just a mention that "One of these days we need to get those nasty old tonsils out of there." What the hell, "One of these days" we might strike oil in the back yard. Right now, watch out for that telephone pole!

∝

Harold said he thought it would hurt like hell to have one's tonsils cut out. I would have to research it a bit with my parents if the
subject came up again, but the spell was broken when Harold, the
human metal detector, made the ultimate find. As we were digging
roadways for our toy cars in the vacant lot, right there where I had
stood and kicked the dirt around a hundred times, Harold found a
gun—a real gun!

We couldn't believe our eyes. There was no mistaking the fact
that this was no toy. It would have been bonanza enough if it had
been, but it was not. It was real!

This gun had been lost or buried for a long time, but we did not
consider that. To us it was a potential murder weapon that had been
buried by a potential murderer. Further, the potential murderer
might be someone living in the neighborhood, perhaps on Pacific
Lane!

First we had to decide whom we would share our secret with.
We wanted to tell someone, but we agreed it should not be an adult.
We could easily lose possession of our great treasure. It was akin to
finding the Mona Lisa. If we let it be known, it was automatically
lost.

Actually, it was Harold's great treasure, but subtly I avoided the
subject of specific ownership and attempted to create the idea of a
partnership. I needed some degree of active involvement, not just for
status purposes; I needed fondling rights. I wanted to hold that gun
in my hands, feel its potential power and imagine its untold stories.
To my great relief, Harold had no problem sharing. It was too big for
any one kid to keep to himself. After all, if the gun was a clue leading
to a murderer, better to share the peril that an innocent discoverer
might find himself assuming with at least one other person. We
sensed danger and our imaginations fueled exaggeration.

We shared our news with Boo, who was not an excitable type.
Nevertheless this was definitely not an ordinary revelation. Consequently, Boo was pretty hyped—for Boo, that is. So we swore him to
secrecy.

After we all calmed down a bit, we decided that we needed to determine who the murderer was and who had been murdered.

House by house, we eliminated the least likely candidates in an attempt to narrow the field down to one frightening and mysterious finalist. Harold said Gloria had all the characteristics needed to be a murderer, but he would have known if she had owned a gun. Besides, the gun looked like it had been in the ground for some years (a fact we really didn't want to consider) and Gloria was only about ten years old. Still, Harold was not ready to discard her as a suspect. He had experienced her homicidal attempts on his own life, he reminded us. What if the BB gun had been a real rifle? Harold had a point. We had all witnessed Gloria's murderous temper, but we all knew that the only person Gloria wanted to kill was Harold, and he was among us, hale and hearty. Gloria was not our killer.

Boo's father, Mr. Knappenberger, had to be among the nominees, since he, an avid hunter, owned guns and knew how to shoot things. Boo was not pleased with this premise, and after only minor consideration, we agreed that he was just too nice to be our man. Still, he did drive a Nash—and you couldn't just discount quirky behavior like that. Boo took a lot of jabs over his dad's preference for Nash cars. Boo threatened to pull out of the "secret gun society" unless we discontinued incriminating his father, so we decided to move along.

By now everyone knew that my dad had a tough reputation—mainly as a result of my stories about his exploit in Chadron, but my dad hated guns, and we had only recently arrived in California. The gun had been in the ground long before our arrival. It didn't take Dick Tracy to recognize that.

We had Lucky smell the gun and then followed her all over the neighborhood, hoping obviously that the bloodhound instinct extended to the rat terrier, but it became apparent that Lucky was not on the trail of our killer when she settled down in front of a gopher hole to wait for a wrong move by the industrious burrowing rodent. Put your money on the dog, was my thought, but Lucky lost a bit of status briefly that day. Harold and Boo were pretty unimpressed.

One of our better ideas as amateur detectives was to focus on people we didn't like. A common sight around 7:00 p.m. was Mr. Carter, with his very uncertain step, coming down the alley on his way home. Mr. Carter was usually pretty much in the bag, having spent some two and a half hours in the beer joint across from the steel mill. He kind of frightened us because he looked pretty wild by the time he reached our neighborhood, and he would try to talk to us—I think only to practice some verbal lucidity before reaching home and the probable wrath of Mrs. Carter. Excellent suspect, Mr. Carter. We would have to follow him the next time he came by; perhaps he would try to bury another murder weapon, or even more important, lead us to the murder victim. We had our prime suspect, but who had he killed?

There was a dead gopher on the back step when I got home.

✖

My dad and I had an important junket to make. The time had come to examine some bikes—to determine the objective. It was time to check on the price of a good new bike.

The Western Auto Supply store where my mother worked was in the town of Redondo Beach. Visiting her at work was a double treat—the store was only some seventy-five to one hundred yards from the beach, which I loved from the first moment I set eyes on it. Secondly, I could feel and touch the bike I coveted so—the bike that would soon be mine. A genuine Western Flyer.

I discovered that Western Auto had Western Flyers in three price ranges: Economy, Special, and Deluxe.

The Economy was handsome enough for someone who wanted a bike as badly as I did. The Special had a "tank" with a battery-operated horn and headlight. It was two-tone—metallic gray and blue—and beautiful. It had a price tag of twenty-five dollars, seven dollars more than the Economy model.

The Deluxe bike was so spectacular it was blinding. The price was astronomical as well—forty-four dollars. Forget that! The Special was more bike than I had ever dreamed of owning, and forty-four dollars was enough to retire on, it seemed to me.

My dad told me to consider the prices and tell him which bike I thought I could afford, since half the price was to come from my magazine earnings. This was serious stuff. Dare I dream beyond the Economy model? If I failed to save enough for the Special, would I still qualify for the Economy? No, my father advised me, the bike I chose would be an all or nothing proposition since it would be placed on a "layaway" plan. We would be committed, and I either raised the dough or I continued walking.

I touched the Economy and caressed the Special. I didn't even bother with the Deluxe. I hoped for a sign from my dad, but none seemed forthcoming. Yet I began to get the feeling that he wanted me to reach a bit, to aspire to more than just a bike. He wanted me to display some spunk.

I looked into his eyes as I indicated that I wanted to go for the Special. My choice met with his approval. He smiled and gave me a pat on the back. Then he called my mother's boss over and the metallic gray and blue beauty went on the layaway plan. I had twelve dollars and fifty cents to raise by my birthday. I had an empty feeling in my stomach, but I was excited and happy. How could a birthday seem far away and close at the same time? I had my work cut out for me.

☧☧

One evening at dinner my dad brought up two serious subjects at once: my tonsils and camp. The connection was, he said, that "We are going to have to get rid of the tonsils" before I went off to camp, where my parents wouldn't be around to care for my sore throat, and did I want to go to camp or not?

Well, sure I wanted to go to camp, but Harold had warned that he thought it would hurt a lot, I told my dad, and I could do without a lot of pain, thank you very much!

My mother overheard and joined the discussion. She could see my dad would attempt to require a display of courage on my part. Her approach was different. She explained that I would be sound asleep and would feel nothing during "the little operation." I began to relax. My mother was very trustworthy, and I knew she loved me very much. I was her only kid, and she and my dad were always ready to defend me against any danger. I was safe, tonsils or no tonsils. There would be camp, and I would be healthy there.

In the next few weeks my courage would wax and wane. I realized it was important to stay off the subject with Harold. I already had his opinion on tonsillectomies, and I didn't need fuel for my anxiety.

✕

I worried that I could ill afford it, but Harold had convinced me to spend a hard-earned and precommitted dime. We were on our way to a matinee double feature. It was a glorious Sunday and I had sold all my magazines. The dime would get me in, but I would do without popcorn, candy, or pop, which was okay.

For a dime, two movies, maybe Hopalong Cassidy and Gene Autry, or Cagney and Bogart, or Flynn and Gable, Heddy and Lana, or Astaire and Rogers. A newsreel, a cartoon, previews and best of all, a serial—for a dime! The Grand Theater was about a two-mile walk. Boo and Richard were with us, so we talked about our gun and Mr. Carter, the murderer.

Harold told Boo that I was going to have my tonsils out, and Boo said he thought it would hurt like hell. I explained the business about being asleep, but Boo said he doubted he would sleep through such an event, that it would hurt too much and probably bleed a lot. Jesus, I didn't need this.

I changed the subject to camp. Boo and Richard weren't going, and if they were unhappy about it, it didn't show. They had each other, built-in company that Harold and I didn't have. Gloria was in no way a companion to Harold, and I had no brothers or sisters. Harold and I realized they would be fine without camp. The Knappenbergers were a larger and closer-knit family than most we knew.

When we got to the movie the only vacant seats were in the front row, where, we had been warned, "You will ruin your eyes." We were a bit concerned, but the show was too seductive to let the threat of blindness deter us. We risked it.

It was a long time for kids to go without food. Harold, Boo and Richard were in the same boat as I. None of us had any money for refreshments, and the entire program bordered on four hours. But it was a grand four hours, even if we were famished by the time we reached our homes.

The famine ended abruptly at my house, since my grandmother

would never dream of a kitchen without multiple fresh baked dessert items. Swedish grandmothers are a treasure every kid should experience, and the rest of the kids in the neighborhood were the happy beneficiaries of a friend with a Swedish grandmother.

There were occasions when the allure was simply overpowering, like when my grandmother would bake cinnamon rolls, for instance.

Cinnamon rolls are wonderful; they taste almost as good as they smell. As they are baking, they smell better than anything in the world. Coffeecake is the same thing, just a single unit instead of individual units; at least such was true of my grandmother's version.

The aroma would begin to build as my grandmother progressed through the pre-oven preparation, and then, with the application of heat, waft its way throughout the neighborhood, and like nerve gas, render everyone in its path helpless.

People knew they couldn't knock on our door and plead for a sample, but kids were not so easily intimidated—decorum was an unknown trait and incompatible with preadolescent appetites. So Harold, Boo, and Richard could be expected to suggest some excuse to penetrate the vault containing the source of the irresistible aroma.

Everyone was a winner. My grandmother knew my friends had been attracted as a direct result of her baking prowess, and as my friends sat savoring cinnamon rolls and milk, everyone was, at that moment, exactly where they most wanted to be. Norman Rockwell would have painted the scene without changing a single tiny detail; it was perfect.

⊐⊏

While I struggled with the problems of obtaining a bike, a tonsillectomy, and getting to camp, problems were developing in the world—problems of cataclysmic proportion. At the time, we kids were oblivious to the serious side of it all.

Adolf Hitler was presented in a fashion that made him seem like a cartoon character, but on September 1, 1939, he invaded Poland, essentially starting a world war. Italy's dictator, Mussolini, was portrayed as even more clownish; we kids saw no threat at all. There was a war going on in Europe, but in terms of distance, Europe was like another planet to us.

On June 14, 1940, German troops marched into Paris, and even the kids began to see a serious side to it all when we viewed from our seats in the Grand Theater the heartbreaking spectacle of a weeping Parisian man watching the Nazi goosesteppers march through his beloved city. No one who saw it ever forgot that scene.

The prospect of a world war, I must confess, was more exciting than tragic from our point of view. The comic books were already drawing heavily on the Nazis for villainous subject matter. The American adult public may have wanted to avoid war, but the male kid population saw America as invincible, and were eager to see verification of these views.

A fellow named Wendell Wilkie chose to run for president against a seemingly godlike FDR. We kids instantly hated Wilkie. The poor man had a status not much better than Hitler among Pacific Lane residents. FDR was "President Roosevelt" and we kids expected him to be the president forever. As it turned out, he nearly achieved permanent president status, ultimately elected for an unprecedented four terms.

Our parents did not share our attitude about the condition of world affairs. London was being bombed almost daily and the Brits were bombing Berlin in retaliation. Everyone considered England to be America's friend, and so we were, but the idea of joining our friends in a war was not a pleasant prospect to anyone over eighteen. Peoples' lives were just settling down following the long, tough Great Depression and a war sounded like more hardship, including separations among family members. Soon Americans would know the heartbreak of husbands, fathers, and sweethearts departing home and hearth to fight a war. As in any other war, many would never return.

The great, new war machines began to catch the fancies of young boys like myself, especially the airplanes. Newsreels showing Stuka dive bombers and Spitfire fighter planes began to appear on the screens and in magazines and newspapers. Soon we were drawing scenes of dogfights on our notebook paper, which we considered adventurous rather than terrifying. The outcome of our notebook battles was never in doubt, of course. But in reality, the war news of 1940 and '41 was nearly all very, very bad, even though there were brilliant attempts to put a positive spin on things, mainly by

Churchill and Stalin. They were emerging heros who were locked in desperate battles with a seemingly invincible enemy. If there was ever a lesson in history concerning the "never give up" attitude, Great Britain and Russia could serve as the most graphic of examples.

In retrospect, I often think about my nine-year-old counterparts growing up in London, Leningrad, or Berlin. While I was able to view WWII as a great adventure, they were spending horrifying nights huddled and cringing in bomb shelters. A major portion of the world was turning cruel beyond comprehension, but American pre-adolescent kids were focused in an oblique direction, excited. That's how we felt as U.S. involvement became more and more overt, yet so very distant geographically.

The Depression had left people badly scarred—imbued qualities that might have never surfaced if it hadn't been so difficult. It was a crisis that caused people to pull apart instead of pull together. My father was a perfect example: He should have been a happy-go-lucky type, but the hard times produced a suspiciousness, a paranoia that he was never able to shed. He never really found his own lost character.

The problem was synchronous, tragically. At a moment in world history when people needed to set racial, ethnic, and religious differences aside and work things out, they were pointed in the opposite direction because of recent past history.

My dad was afraid the Jews would own everything and have all the money; afraid the Catholics were ruled by the Pope and were breeding to overpower through "out-populating us." Of course the Irish and Italians were Catholics! Blacks were just ignored, considered insignificant at any level.

The point is, my dad's attitude was very common, not only in America, but because the Depression was an economic disaster throughout the world, suspicion was metamorphosing into hatred everywhere. Scapegoats were needed, and there was an ample supply available.

Any minority was a potential scapegoat, and in California, Japanese-Americans were very handy. Mysterious and industrious, they began to be targeted as a group that needed to be somehow controlled. I heard the talk, but my exposure to Japanese-Americans was represented by Chizuko and Sakio primarily, along with a few others I knew, but not as well. No sale! I didn't buy it. I was indebted to those two girls, and I knew I would never have any chance to repay them. My loyalty and friendship were all I could offer. They were unquestionably really nice—period!

This terrible synchronism—the Depression, the paranoia, and the arrival of charismatic sociopaths whose genius was the exploitation of these very unlikely conditions—these coincidental ingredients came close to destroying any hope of a peaceful world. Rather than the meek, the maniacs came close to inheriting the earth. But we Pacific Lane kids did not perceive things that way at all. The eventual outcome was never in doubt for us, and as it turned out, we were right.

⋈

One of our suspects moved out of the neighborhood, leaving only Mr. Carter among active candidates. Mr. and Mrs. Shepherd moved from the house separating Harold and Boo. Mr. Shepherd raised our suspicions because he had no children, an abnormal condition, we thought. Neither Mrs. Shepherd nor any other woman qualified, since no woman could have committed the unspeakable crime the owner of our gun was surely guilty of. We had never seen Mr. Shepherd drunk—a fatal flaw in our case against him, we agreed. We were certain that strong drink would be needed to commit homicide, even with a large inheritance or insurance policy or something like that as a motive.

We had seen Mrs. Carter sweeping her porch, so we knew she was not the victim. She had not been shot to death with our gun. In fact, she had not, from appearances, even been wounded. We had no choice but to follow Mr. Carter and hope for the classic "return to the scene of the crime" syndrome to take place.

This would take some serious planning. For starters, Mr. Carter didn't come our way every day. Additionally, it was usually daylight and he could, if he was at all wary, see us following him. And finally, he was a killer, and while we were a bit skittish about him before, we now would be risking our lives if he suspected we were on to his murderous ways.

We gathered in the vacant lot at the new secret spot where we had sequestered the gun and planned the formation of a DEW (Distant Early Warning) system line. We agreed to rotate surveillance duties at the beer joint. If Mr. Carter came out, the one on duty would run ahead and alert the other two. A good plan and easy to achieve since Mr. Carter was usually weaving from one side of the alley to the other as he made his way home.

Since Boo was the last one in the covert triumvirate, he was assigned the first watch. We went together to find our lookout spot and left Boo to keep an eagle eye on the door. Harold and I left to fondle and play with the gun until Boo arrived to put Phase II in motion.

When Boo did not return for dinner, Harold and I feared the worst—the murderous Mr. Carter must have discovered Boo lurking in the bushes and dispatched him, probably without a trace.

When we heard Knappy calling Boo for dinner, we took off for the stakeout area. Boo was sound asleep in the bushes. Harold and I had not taken into account how laid-back Boo was in comparison to us. He often nodded off reading comic books or even in the middle of a hide-and-seek game. We were irritated but woke him up and hurried him home lest our sleuthing schemes be revealed and our gun discovered.

So the "Three Musketeers" returned to Pacific Lane in time for dinner with no one the wiser—except themselves. Boo would not stand the next watch, it was decided.

***

My parents, it seemed to me, were being more attentive and permissive lately, while at the same time the removal of my tonsils entered the conversation more frequently. "A little trip to the hospital to get those poisonous things out of there" is how it was described. I remained noncommittal, thinking if I did not agree, perhaps the whole subject would just go away. That approach did not seem to be working.

Finally, the rubber hit the road. A date had been set. It had been decided that if I wanted to go to camp (I did, I did), this little business about the tonsils needed to be put behind us. Camp became an incentive; the tonsillectomy became a prerequisite. Trapped like a rat!

Other incentives began to surface. I was told to choose some comic books to save for the hospital stay (hospital *stay*?), and when I asked how many, I was given approval for ten! *Ten*? A dollar's worth of comic books? What was going on here? My brain, which had been pretty much in neutral, began to shift into gear. Either my parents were indulging in serious overkill, or we were embarking on a much more serious proposition than I had prepared myself for.

My grandmother could not do enough for me. The kitchen was full of baked stuff—cakes, pies, cookies, cinnamon rolls, and more in the oven. The aroma was absolutely heavenly. The whole neighborhood was dehydrated from salivating over the scents emanating from our house.

Grandma Ellen was cooking special dinners for me. While the family ate well, I ate like royalty! I was an only child, but this was going beyond being spoiled. I was being fattened up for the kill.

Still, my parents loved me. I never doubted that even for a moment—not even when we disagreed. I knew I was the center of their universe. They would not ever let anything bad happen to me, let alone be a party to it. Besides, Harold and Boo had never had their tonsils out, so what could they know?

For some reason, every mention or discussion of a tonsillectomy included the promise of ice cream or jello afterwards. That sounded okay, but I never suspected they would try to feed me liver or spinach. What was the point here? If it was such a little deal, why was it such a big deal?

ᴈᴆ

I had made a number of visits to Western Auto to visit my future bike. It was kept upstairs in an attic-like area with all the other layaways. It had a tab marked "Sold—Swigart" on it which gave me a secure feeling—with reservation. What a beauty! Most kids I knew with bikes had used ones. When I came rolling by on this baby, heads would turn. My heart ached for January 30th, my tenth birthday, some six months—an eon—away.

ᴈᴆ

The Redondo pier was only a couple of blocks from the store, and Murch, my mother's boss, had walked me down there a couple of times and set me up with a fishing pole, some tackle, and bait. I loved to be there; to my left the breakers rolling to the beach and to my right, the expanse of the great Pacific Ocean stretching to infinity. The only missing ingredient was a fish on the end of my line.

Until now, I had only had one fishing experience, and it had been more unpleasant than entertaining. Prior to our move we had gone to visit my mother's sister, Stella, and her husband, Bill, in Norfolk, Nebraska. They were avid fisherpeople. My parents, by contrast, didn't even care for fish as a meal.

At my request, we were fishing. The adults would much rather have been visiting, catching up on a few years of separation while the Depression raged on and everyone concentrated on survival.

While my aunt, uncle, and dad did some catching up, my mom and I fished from a little rickety old bridge only three or four feet above the small creek.

What happened then was most unlikely. A trout of serious size decided, for no reason anyone could explain later, to swallow our worm—which of course disguised the deadly hook within.

All hell broke loose! My mother had never caught a fish; neither, of course, had I. But in only moments, the glistening, flopping rainbow trout was on the bridge, and we faced the task, my mother decided, of killing it. She was certain that the next step was to prevent its escape and end its misery. It had to be killed.

While my mom held the fish down, I was sent to find a rock of perfect size to smash its brain. Ye gods, this was what people found so great about fishing? My mother was convinced this was an act of benevolent euthanasia; I wasn't so sure. The fish sure knew otherwise.

I delivered a stone, perfect for the deed, and put one foot on the victim's tail as directed. My mother delivered the first blow. She was not adept at this sort of thing and the blow landed more mid-body than she intended. I removed my foot and the fish flopped.

I put my foot back in place, but with some anxiety regarding my toes; the stone moved through an arc, and my foot jerked back. The blow landed once again on the mid-portion of a rapidly deteriorating, once impressive fish. The combination of my mother's poor aim and the animal's movement had conspired to apparently save its life, but at a gruesome price, as the fish unquestionably moved once again.

At this point my mother decided on a series of quick blows, which she vigorously delivered—some finding their mark, some wide, some short. It mattered little what part of the fish received a blow.

The fish at last remained motionless, but it bore little resemblance to the animal that only minutes ago swam freely in the cold waters beneath the tiny bridge. It was a slimy, bloody mess.

The rest of the group arrived on the scene to find us staring at the mess we had made. They too began to stare in wonder.

My mother explained, citing our unexpected luck and her understanding of the need to kill the poor unfortunate fish. It was literally purée.

My uncle held the fish up by the tail—about all that was identifiable—and the trio began to chuckle. Soon they were overcome with laughter, and we realized that we had given new meaning to the term "overkill."

It was a fish story that would resurface many times over the years. My mother, always a good sport, laughed with the rest.

But I was some years older now and had done some observing since the "trout incident," and fishing off the Redondo pier with the great Pacific before me seemed a wonderful pastime.

The fish everyone on the pier was after was halibut. One or two of these twenty- to thirty-pound giants would be caught a day. A variety of other fish were caught as well, but the objective remained halibut.

I never seemed to get a nibble. I watched others yell for the net to be lowered by rope to bring their catch the twenty-five feet to pier level from where we cast our lines, but I never seemed to be stationed in the lucky spot.

I decided to do some research on the matter. I left my pole and line securely braced in case the impossible should happen, and I went on a quest for knowledge.

Two old-timers were side by side some twenty or thirty yards from my spot, and one look told all: these old boys knew from fishing; they also looked approachable.

I approached. I laid it right on the line. "Why," I asked, "can I never seem to catch one of those spectacular halibut fishes? What is the secret? How can I succeed?"

The two men looked at each other and came up with an answer that was both simple and sage. "A good fisherman never leaves his pole" was their advice. A dual purpose had been served; their advice was valid and they were rid of a kid and what might have been a never-ending stream of questions.

I returned to my pole and gripped it firmly in both hands, the end sticking out from my armpit. I sighted down the pole and awaited the anticipated "strike" (big fish talk).

After some minutes it happened: my pole bounced like the granddaddy of all halibut had swallowed my bait and decided to swim to San Diego with it. I was too surprised to react, and before I could, the whole thing repeated itself.

Knowing the big fish to be securely hooked, I called for the net. "I've got one, I've got one. Get the net," I yelled. I looked to both sides of me. Everyone was looking at me but no one was moving. Terrified that I might lose this monster, I yelled again, "Get the net." Still no one moved, and it was then I noticed they were all smiling and beginning to chuckle. What the hell was this?

I caught movement out of the corner of my eye and turned completely to my rear. I was face to face with my dad and Murch. Murch had bumped my pole from behind with his hand, which had felt to me, inexperienced with halibut strikes, to be just what I had been waiting for. They were both smiling, but my face was ablaze with embarrassment. I wanted to die.

Murch was a sweet, sensitive man and my dad was a man who could never stand to be laughed at or humiliated. How could they have done this to me?

I dropped the pole on the pier and took off running for the store—away from my humiliation. I ran to my mother for comfort and burst into tears for the first time in ages. She was desperate to know what was wrong but I couldn't tell her. I wanted to hide from everyone—especially my dad and Murch.

Shortly they returned with the fishing gear, looking very sheep-ish. The practical joke had been too successful. The result was far beyond their expectations, and they now felt just awful. They had overstepped and knew how hurt I was. Their hangdog looks did not save them from the wrath of my mother. They got a proper chewing out before they had a chance to apologize, which they were fully prepared to do.

Before their chance came, my mother explained to me that they had made a mistake, and that mistakes were part of life too. She advised me that they now felt as bad as I did, and that they would soon apologize. I would, she said, exhibit maturity if I could forgive their mistake and accept their apology, but God, I didn't want to even think about it, I was so mad and embarrassed.

She soothed me and held me until the pain subsided then called the two contrite perpetrators and told them we were ready to listen. When I saw that they were damned near in tears themselves, my resentment fell away. My dad was not a man who got tears in his eyes. It was a sight I had never seen before.

All was forgiven, but it was a long time before I felt I could fish on the pier again—or even walk out there. Who wants to catch a damned old ugly, smelly fish anyway?

⊐⊏

I had just finished a chocolate malt in record time. Harold had challenged me to see who could finish first and had let me win on purpose. Now I had nothing to do but watch him savor his, the rat!

Harold's mother, Anna, was waiting on a shop full of teenage kids while Howdy tried to keep up with the orders. There was no chance. Anna had to do double duty: Howdy, the grill; Anna, the fountain and the customers. If someone from Hollywood had walked in, they would have expected to find Andy Hardy and Polly there planning to put on a show. The place was so stereotypical of the day.

A main difference was that no one danced there. There was a jukebox for sure, but there was no room to dance. Round tables filled the floor space from the soda fountain counter and stools to the walls in all directions.

Rather than wait for Harold to finish his malt, since he was making an all-day project out of it, or so it seemed, I decided to pick out my ten comic books for the tonsil thing that was pending. Maybe that would get to Harold a bit.

Among the popular books was "Sheena, Queen of the Jungle"—a gorgeous jungle girl dressed in a scanty tiger skin which just barely covered her private parts. For some reason I found myself more and more interested in that comic book while Superman and Batman were losing ground.

A new family had moved into the Shepherd house, adding to the kid population a nine-year-old girl named Jovine. She liked to go shirtless these warm summer days, and I found that bothered me for some reason. The reason seemed somehow related to Sheena. I decided to give that more thought sometime soon and paid Anna the dollar for the ten comic books (no, no sales tax in 1941). Harold was wide-eyed, but I avoided his questions by offering to let him read them—no strings attached. Harold tended to use things like comic books as bartering bait. He was satisfied, and the subject of tonsils, about which I already had more input from Harold than I wanted, had been averted.

In all the Sheena adventures, she wound up rescuing the handsome but inept white hunter, Bill. I felt I should find this female dominance repugnant, but for some reason I found it kind of fascinating. What was happening here?

⋈

It might seem like a nine-and-a-half-year-old boy should know all about the birds and the bees, but I didn't. None of the kids in the neighborhood did either. It was not a topic we had dealt with.

One afternoon as I walked the alley alone, trying to find something a la "Harold the metal detector," I was hailed by a kid a bit older than I who lived about halfway to Howdy's. A nice enough guy but seemingly not very interested in sports or games, so he was not a "regular." He had something to show me, he said, and after making certain we were not being watched, he produced a comic book of a variety I had not seen before. He called it a Tijuana comic book.

For the uninitiated, the comic book was about two inches wide and about four inches long, containing about ten pages, black and white. But what a ten pages it contained! I thumbed through it completely puzzled by what I saw and finally asked the big question, "What are they doing?" It looked absolutely ridiculous.

The kid's name was Dean Wickham, and he didn't act like I was dumb. It was more like he realized he had information to convey and he did it in a concise manner.

"That," he informed me, "is how babies are made by husbands and wives."

Without hesitation, I knew he was dead wrong. The idea that my mother and dad had indulged in such a ridiculous and obscene act was ludicrous—an obvious hoax, an attempt by an older kid to make a younger kid believe a stupid story. I was not buying it, no way!

Dean, however, stuck to his guns and put my mind to heavy thought on the matter. It came to me—the proof it couldn't be so. I informed him that my Aunt Miller had a son and she was not married, therefore, no such liaison could have occurred.

Shaking his head he concluded that I was just too dumb to waste any more time on, not to mention that he had expected me to be excited by the forbidden and elicit book and I had just chosen to deny the obvious. We headed off in opposite directions.

Troubled by it all I headed home with the image of what Popeye was doing to Olive Oyl fresh in my mind. I decided to test the theory. As I helped myself to a sugar cookie baked earlier in the day, I casually asked my mother if Aunt Miller was married. Her answer was a K.O. punch. She said, "Of course she's married. Billy's her son. Billy's dad is at work when we visit."

Bingo! Just what I didn't want to hear: the verification that 1+1=3, and my parents had indeed indulged in this perverse behavior, and I was the living, breathing proof. My mother never knew what she had revealed to me.

Now I knew why I was an only child. Anyone who knew my mother knew she would never get in such a position *twice*! Even once was hard to imagine, but never twice. Why, I wondered, wasn't my mother embarrassed to have me around if I represented such a perverse act? I never knew what the immaculate conception was all about. Now I thought maybe I was one.

Instead of brooding about it, I decided to develop a more intimate relationship with Sheena. Perhaps another look at Dean's

Tijuana comic book was worth consideration too, and what was wrong with a girl going without a shirt if she wanted to? Maybe, I thought, Jovine might be willing to educate me a bit more relative to our comparative anatomy. From this day of unfolding mysteries, I would view girls differently.

⚏

"T" day was approaching like ground rush to a sky diver, and before I knew it, I was all dressed up and headed with my parents to the hospital.

Once checked in, wouldn't you know, I was instructed to take my clothes *off!* I had gotten all dressed up for a car ride to the hospital. Great logic!

The bed I was to lie on was ten feet off the ground, it seemed to me. I felt like I was scaling a sheer cliff. At the summit, I found myself sitting on sheets stretched so tight I hardly dented the surface of the bed. I was in a perilous place. Even the bed was dangerous.

Who would be coming into this room, I wondered? I was not very presentable, I was in this gown and it didn't cover much of me. Sitting as I was, it ended above mid-thigh, and if I had to get up, I meant to keep my back to the wall; nothing was covered in the rear! I was apprehensive enough without being made to look like a fool. This was an experience we needed to get over and finished as soon as possible. The stack of comic books did not interest me, my buns were exposed, and I was very uncomfortable.

I was about to ask my parents what comes next when my mother began to deliver what sounded to me like a prepared speech. She told me as soon as the doctor got those "two little tabs" out of my throat, it would be all over. I would be asleep during the whole thing, and when I woke up I could have as much ice cream or jello as I wanted. I had heard a lot about jello and ice cream. Every time the subject of tonsils came up, it seemed we would be talking about ice cream and jello, jello and ice cream. Ice cream at Howdy's sounded a lot better to me than ice cream in a hospital.

I was getting more nervous. I couldn't think of "tabs" anywhere on my body that I would want cut off, and what was so bad about tonsils anyway? This was really a lot of fuss for a couple of "little tabs." I was not having fun. Harold's remark was never far from my worried thoughts.

My dad was now contributing his share, wanting me to be a man about it all. When I wanted to be treated like a grownup, I was reminded I was still a kid. Now I wanted to act like a kid and they wanted a grownup. The classic no-win situation. Let's go home!

A nurse entered the room with an armful of stuff and I squeezed my knees tighter together. It seemed to me the view under the "gown" was right at her eye level, thanks to this platform I was sitting on. I wanted some privacy.

The nurse walked over to me and I couldn't believe what she told me to do. I had been raised among people who were really modest about nudity, but this nurse wanted me to lie on my side facing away from her. Did she realize what would be revealed?

I looked at my mother. Surely she would intervene and explain to the nurse that the gown failed to supply proper coverage in back, but instead she gave me a nod that indicated I was to comply.

My eyes got hot, and before anyone could see that they were welling up, I lay down, rolled over and assumed a fetal position, which was just what the nurse wanted. I surrendered and awaited further humiliation.

Something was inserted back there and I closed my eyes. Why couldn't I just disappear like Mandrake the Magician? As if by magic, that's just about what happened.

It was as if I had disappeared. I felt like I was trying to materialize and my image wouldn't quite join my being. Finally, we merged. I thought I was back from some journey, but it was night and I couldn't see where I had come to. I was alone, a condition totally unfamiliar to me. I had never been alone before, except in the bathroom.

I tried to call out for my parents. Good Lord, I wasn't totally blind, I discovered, but I realized my throat must have been cut! I croaked like a frog and tasted blood. Or was it burning gasoline? Fuzzy images began to form and I could hear my mother's voice far off in the distance. I wasn't alone. Thank God!

But I was afraid to try to talk again. I still felt the pain of my last attempt and couldn't muster the courage to risk that pain again.

A complication was developing; I had to urinate. The urge was developing fast and I now realized I was in a bed—where and for what reason I couldn't piece together. I had to chance it; I needed to go!

From a raw, ravaged throat I croaked out my developing emergency to my mother, who was now beginning to come into focus. She responded soothingly that I really didn't have to go to the bathroom—"It just feels like you do." Now what the hell did that mean? I was over nine years old, not some recently toilet-trained little child. What was going on? I knew when I had to go, for Christ's sake.

Before events got too desperate I decided to take things into my own hands, literally. We little boys pinched our penises to help postpone urination—a natural method in an emergency.

I had to make my way through an unexpected barrier of cloth, and when I grasped my penis, I immediately forgot my throat; but when I screamed, I quickly remembered it again. Good Lord, I hurt everywhere.

Everything was visually clear now, and while I watched, a nurse removed a mountain of cotton from my private area. My anxiety was so great there was no room for the usual embarrassment I should have felt.

As the cotton was peeled away, I began to see bloody cotton, and then, my bloody little nine-year-old penis. What had happened to it?

My mother was droning on about cleanliness, but I couldn't make the connection. There was something about filth and disease— "a greater peril than the tonsils," and "it was the perfect opportunity." Apparently they had removed yet another flap of skin "for my own good," my mother assured me.

I looked at my dad, but he was letting my mother do the talking and didn't want to make eye contact.

I wondered if I really saw what I thought I saw. After all, I had been rendered unconscious somehow, and perhaps I had hallucinated—only thought I had been mutilated. But the pain emanating from down there spoke for itself, and I was now rebandaged and unable to examine my wounded, formerly private, now quite public, part.

A sense of betrayal was welling up in me. I was afraid to cry, knowing that my throat, raw meat, would hurt a lot worse if I did. Besides, my father didn't like me to be a cry baby, and it just seemed too late to cry about all this anyway. I had no idea what had been done to me, but the image of the exposed bud-like head of my penis seemed major to me.

My mind drifted to the only positive thing I could think of: ice cream and jello. It was a relief to my parents, who felt a return to normal by way of my request. When the ice cream arrived, I tried to eat a bit, but my throat hurt too bad to swallow anything. Besides, it was the wrong use for ice cream. What would really feel good, I thought, would be to stick my bloody little penis in the nice, cool, rapidly melting glop.

Would my throat ever feel normal again? I wondered. And what of my poor little member with its now-exposed rosy little head? What could be cleaner and healthier about that?

One thing was certain—I wouldn't be thinking about Sheena for a while. My eyes were burning again, so I closed them, rolled over and summoned sleep. I had learned a new word today: "circumcision."

☒

I would definitely be going to camp!

The tonsillectomy-circumcision and school year were behind me. I had succeeded at one and survived the other, barely. Kids are flexible and survive situations adults would never get through without being seriously scarred, physically and psychologically.

The tonsillectomy-circumcision had left my parents feeling guilty and worried that they had handled things badly. They had listened to the doctor, thinking his advice was a result of his great experience and wisdom. Their parental intuition would have served us all better, but this was the age of tonsillectomies and circumcisions and God–Doctor belief. Each decade would have its anatomical scapegoats. Tonsils, foreskins, uteri, breasts, appendixes, ovaries—not to mention the displacement of natural childbirth by caesarian section. When are we going to learn that doctors are dangerous? And greedy.

I've learned! I don't need to lose a limb in the process. Those two tabs and a flap were plenty, thank you very much. From now on

I would listen to Harold. What *he* had said about the tonsillectomy turned out to be the best information I received.

I was damned glad we would be at camp together. His camp experience would be needed. I was too "camp ignorant"; he had the "camp savvy."

Harold was also next in line to stand watch. Our murder investigation had gone on hold while I recuperated. Only the tonsillectomy was discussed with the neighborhood kids. The circumcision was never leaked to the general population. Harold would have fainted.

∞

As we installed Harold on the stakeout, we gave Boo a bad time about his performance on the first watch. He shrugged; waiting and watching were boring, he advised us.

We were all beginning to feel that the investigation needed to be concluded soon. We began to wonder if we might be doing something wrong by not sharing the gun information with our parents. Additionally, this caper was keeping us from group fun with the other kids. Our nine-year-old attention spans were beginning to evaporate a bit, and I kind of wanted to get to know Jovine a little better. A shirtless summer would not last forever.

When Mr. Carter finally came by again, we were not manning our DEW line position. Nevertheless, we sprang into action! We dove for cover, although in his condition it was just as likely that he wouldn't even notice had we been standing five feet in front of him. As he weaved his way past us, I realized time had eroded the edge from our imaginary serial killer's menacing appearance. Mr. Carter just didn't look dangerous. He just looked drunk, which was normal for him.

But our spirits rose and our collective pulses skipped a beat as Mr. Carter stopped, looked each direction, and disappeared behind a wooden stand on which rested some six or seven large garbage cans. We had been ready to give up too soon; something sinister was going on because there was no logical, legal reason to go back there.

We waited. We waited and waited. We waited some more. No Mr. Carter emerged. Someone was going to have to get close enough to see what was going on back there. We moved closer. We watched, we listened. Nothing!

The building abutting the area was a one-level, flat-roofed, multiple garage. We knew how to get onto the roof and finally decided to sneak up there where we could get a view of Mr. Carter, probably in some dastardly act. When we crept to the edge and looked over, we saw Mr. Carter sitting against the garage wall and there was something dead beside him—a dead soldier. The "dead soldier" was an empty whiskey bottle, and Mr. Carter was dead drunk and sound asleep. Some serial killer!

We had wasted a lot of prime play time on this caper, and had no story to tell that might have made us neighborhood heroes. It was time to show the gun to a parent and risk losing it, or be able to play with it in the open—the ultimate "cops and robbers" equipment.

Because Boo's dad was the neighborhood "gun dad," we chose to present our once-in-a-lifetime find to him for a reaction. The gun was far too corroded, he pointed out, to supply any clues in respect to its possible criminal involvement. Additionally, because the trigger, the hammer and firing pin, ammo clip, and spring return were all missing, it was probably less dangerous than a cap gun. The gun was ours to keep. "Have fun," he said.

In games requiring guns we took turns. It was always to be the "good guy gun." The kids in the neighborhood were as impressed as we had been when we made our discovery. We got a lot of mileage out of the gun, as we had expected and hoped we would. No hero status, but plenty of envy. We soaked it up.

Mr. Carter was acquitted, found innocent of all charges.

ᴐᴄ

The big vacant lot next to my uncle's house was an entire playground. It became almost anything we needed it to be at any given time.

In addition to the iceplant monster and the secret caves, we made roads in the dirt for our toy cars and a battleground for our toy soldiers. It was common to discover a horned lizard buried in the soft, sandy topsoil. We called them "horny toads." The phrase had no sexual connotation in the 1940s, at least not to our knowledge. These youthful games gave way to more sophisticated games as our play activities matured.

In our cave, the hole with boards over the top, which we improved with a layer of cardboard to seal the cracks and a layer of dirt to disguise and validate the "cave" designation, we had candles for illumination, and ultimately there was an old Jack Emerson-donated *Sunshine and Health* magazine. The magazine shed little light on the vast sea of ignorance that we sought to reduce. Pornography was illegal; *Sunshine and Health* was not. The pictures were maddeningly two-dimensional, and no viewing angle provided anything more than we already knew. We tried, but it was hopeless.

We hit fly balls with baseballs that would ultimately lose the cover and require being re-covered with friction tape. It worked just fine—a bit sticky at first.

We set up targets and shot our BB guns at bottles and cans. The Daisy "Red Rider" model air rifle was the top of the line. There were only two models. With the exception of Gloria Chapman, no one ever fired a BB gun at anybody, or even pointed one at anybody. It was the universal condition of ownership. Gloria didn't own a BB gun; she shot Harold with his own gun. Why he kept it loaded was a mystery.

In addition to horny toads, red ants populated the vacant lot with many colonies. They were not very good natured.

During a session of road building with Harold, I became very uncomfortable. I gave myself a rub, but the discomfort did not diminish, and in another moment I realized the discomfort was intensifying, soon reaching the point of outright pain. I set sail for home and burst through the back door, through the kitchen and into the bathroom.

In almost a single motion, I had my pants and underwear down, exposing my recently mutilated body part. Attached to the now-exposed, unprotected, rosy little underdeveloped bud-like tip was a red ant, hanging on for dear life with its pincers, the rosy bud looking considerably redder as the ant's legs pawed the air. Had the ant sensed my circumcised condition as I played in the dirt of the vacant lot?

My parents and the doctor should see this! Would kids have their foreskins amputated if they knew of the red ant peril that preyed on recently circumcised boys? I should hope not.

The problem was not solved, only discovered. I now had to get the damned thing off, and I worried that the devil ant would only turn on my fingers if I tried to pull it off.

Pain transcended fear, and with thumb and forefinger, I gently pulled, only causing the ant to increase its mandibular grip, which proportionately increased the pain.

We kind of feared that if you harmed a red ant, their relatives all knew it, so we were reluctant to kill them, but this one had to die, and right now.

The ant was disemboweled in a piece of toilet paper, and although his grip was now a bona fide death grip, I pulled him off my poor throbbing little member. It stung like hell and brought tears to my eyes as I dropped the tissue with the squashed ant into the toilet. Had I cursed myself in addition to my wound? Would I be forced to abandon any future vacant lot play—and would that be enough? Would they perhaps march into the house and attack me in my bed while I slept? I had never heard of anything happening to that degree, but I decided to avoid the vacant lot for a while. Even if the stories had some truth, surely an ant's memory, considering its obvious lack of brain size, would be limited. I would go with that, but I still felt like a foreskin would have been an advantage in all this. I had yet to see any advantage to circumcision.

From a safe distance I called to Harold, who was engrossed in road building. This was an ideal time for some serious comic book reading on his front stoop, where I could see them coming if they launched an attack en masse; I didn't want to risk another assault on my very tender little member.

✄

While the vacant lot was both a multifaceted game and the arena as well, our activities reached past its borders to embrace every appropriate part of the neighborhood. We had lots to do and we needed room to do it all. Many of our games seem to have disappeared, replaced by organized sports and electronics. Our games were better.

"Work-up" and "hit the bat" were offshoots of baseball, but required fewer people and less space. We utilized our vacant lot and alley respectively.

A fielder "worked up" by catching a fly ball hit by the batter, who served as his own pitcher, and attempted to hit fly balls the fielders couldn't catch. When the fielder caught three, the fielder became the batter and the batter became the fielder. Four people were ample for a game of "work-up."

"Hit the bat" was played in the alley, and instead of fly balls, the batter hit ground balls. A team consisted of only two players, with a maximum of three. The idea was to field the ground ball and freeze in place. The batter then placed the bat on the pavement laterally, and stood behind it.

Now the fielder, from the precise spot he collected the ball, rolled it toward the batter in an attempt to hit the prone bat. If the ball missed or hit the bat but did not bounce over it, the batter remained the batter. If it bounced over the bat and was not caught before bouncing again, a new batter had emerged.

They were great games, allowing us to develop some feel for the game of baseball without a diamond or all the people needed for the real thing. Early on, the bat was almost more than we could handle, but we grew and the bat didn't.

A favorite coed game was "kick the can," a game that often included everyone in the neighborhood, and for some reason, was usually played toward dusk and into darkness. If you never played this game, you definitely had an incomplete childhood, and if you don't know how it is played, you must be young or an immigrant. Essentially, it is just a variation of "hide-and-seek." The only addition is a piece of equipment called a tin can.

As in the basic hide-and-seek game, one person was "it" and the others hid.

Once spotted, "hider" and "it" raced to the tin can. If the "hider" won, he had the option of being "free" by jumping over the can or kicking the can, forcing "it" to retrieve and replace it while the kicker hid again. If "it" won the race, the loser, of course, was "it."

We had cap guns, but we rarely had caps. Caps came in sheets for single-shot guns and boxes of five rolls for the repeater guns, which never worked very well, but we felt grateful when we had them because they contributed to the reality of "cops and robbers" and "cowboys and Indians." A half-inch square piece of red paper with a gray dot of gunpowder in the center—that was a "cap."

We Pacific Laners, namely Harold, Boo, and I, felt we invented "Superman" as a game. Played in warm weather, the only required props were a bathing suit (bathing suits fit like jockey shorts in the '40s), a towel, and a safety pin. The towel was the essential attire for superheroing; it became "the cape." The cape was an absolutely inspirational and imperative accessory. Without it there was no chance of super activities.

We were all on the side of good; there was no evil Superman in our games. We mostly just ran around trying to make our capes trail in typical Superman fashion. It was hard to achieve and harder yet to know if we had. We were trying to fly, of course.

We rarely had to be shooed outside. Except for our devotion to comic books, our whole world was outside. It was where we wanted to be.

And how much parental involvement was there in our games? Absolutely none! Somehow we had fun anyway.

Harold broke his arm! He fell off his beat-up old wobbly bike, and when he collected himself, his arm was broken.

Harold's status in the neighborhood soared. He got to wear a sling with his arm in a cast, and he played it to the hilt, the lucky devil.

We often pretended "broken arm" so we could wear a sling, but this was the real thing. I was impressed and envious. We all were. In fact, I was so envious I didn't ask him how much it hurt, even though I really wanted to know. He had the spotlight.

This broken arm could have far-reaching consequences for me, however. I knew that camp had been paid for and was nonrefundable, except in emergency situations. I sensed an emergency situation for Harold, but it was unlikely his emergency would stretch to include me. Camp departure was five days away. Was I worried? You bet I was! I badly needed a confederate for this camp business; there was too much I didn't know.

Harold's absence from the neighborhood was the main—no, make that the *only* reason—I wanted to go to camp. If he was going, I wanted to go. Would he still go with a broken arm of less than a week's duration? My mind said no problem; my stomach sent a much different message.

In the excitement of it all, Harold had not thought about the impact of his glorious broken bone on the pending trip to camp. Would we be together at Little Green Valley? The jury was out and I desperately needed a verdict. The prospect of camp with no one who knew the ropes, or worse, no one I even knew, was not an appealing situation.

I tried to remain optimistic, since Harold really wanted to go. Perhaps, I thought, that would constitute the central criterion in the decision process, but alas, Anna's phone call confirmed my newest nightmare. I would be going to camp without Harold.

Harold thought he felt as bad as I did, but there was no way. For Harold it was disappointment, for me it was disaster. How did I get into these horrible situations?

Still, according to Harold, who had sold me on the camp program to begin with, we were going because it was fun. I wasn't, after all, going to Alcatraz. Think positively, I told myself. Things would work out okay. The feeling in my stomach persisted as the hour of departure seemed to be approaching at the speed of light. *Fun*, I told myself. It was going to be *fun*. Oh boy, camp!

⚎

Magazine sales would have to wait a couple of weeks while I did camp. Harold would now be assisting Boo to cover my regular customers and whatever else they could sell. It occurred to me that Harold's broken arm could be very good for sales. Of course the profits would be theirs, but I would have to remember to check this out. Perhaps an arm in a sling would put me over the top in a hurry—removing a major worry from my life. My contribution was coming along okay, but some acceleration wouldn't hurt anything. The image of my beautiful layaway bike was never out of my thoughts for long.

I had myself pretty well under control and resigned to Y camp.

My memory of the Sierra country was vivid—a most pleasant memory of the most beautiful place I had ever seen. I had hoped to see the mountains again and here was my chance. My stomach actually felt a bit better when I directed my thoughts along these lines.

The prospect of riding on a bus added a bit to the adventure, since I really never had occasion to go anywhere on a bus. It looked like fun. I always kind of envied the kids who rode to school on the bus, although I thought they were probably poor and had to live a long way from school. Anyway, Harold said we would sing songs on the bus. That would be a leg up for me since I could sing any song I had ever heard—well enough for others to stop singing and listen. Mainly adults were impressed, not kids. Kids never listened; they just sang, whether they could carry a tune or not. It usually sounded awful.

So this was it! I was on the bus, my sleeping bag and suitcase were in the baggage compartment, and I was ready for the singing. Mom, Dad, and Lucky were there to see me off. Mom's eyes were burning, but she knew she couldn't let herself cry. That could pull the rug out from under us all. My dad was acting brave but we all realized this was our first separation and it was a very big deal. But the crowd around us forced a dignity we would rather have ignored and released our emotions. Even Lucky looked worried, and she was. Her dog's brain could pick up on the peculiar events developing here. Her boy was going away somewhere and everyone was nervous.

Harold was right. The singing started as the bus began to move. It is hard to cry and sing at the same time, and the real pros know this. Fifty kids were urged to join in the "Row, Row, Row Your Boat" song as waving parents disappeared from view. It would be a long ten days before kids and parents would be reunited. We soon shifted into a lively but awful sounding chorus of "You Are My Sunshine." Little Green Valley, here come some of the worst young Christian singers ever heard.

The trip to camp was fun. I sang with all the gusto I could muster, and as we headed into the foothills, I really began to think this whole Y camp episode would be a success. My shaky stomach was not even noticeable as the bus downshifted to compensate for the increasing incline of the road. The kids on the bus were rowdy and everyone seemed to know somebody else. I recognized no face among the passengers and no one approached me. Still, there were a number of buses in the caravan, and I suspected there would be a surprise familiar face on one of them once we arrived at Little Green Valley. If not, I would simply watch for another lonely looking, friendless kid and strike up a conversation. It would be okay, I told myself. The scenery infused me with optimism and confidence.

The mountains loomed ahead, and shrubs gave way to trees, which in turn gave way to really big trees. The mountains were as beautiful as I recalled from our migratory trip from Nebraska a couple of years earlier. This was wonderful. If camp was as good as the bus trip, it would be great. My anxieties had fallen away completely, placing me in a most vulnerable condition.

⌘

The buses labored under their load and the increasing grade. I wondered how many gears were available to the driver. It seemed to me he had downshifted a dozen times and we were really creeping now—barely moving, but moving. The driver did not seem concerned, so I continued to enjoy the beautiful scenery.

Now the stress of the grade eased and soon the driver was more concerned with too much speed as we dove toward the valley floor. He was definitely working harder at this point than he had been during our tortoise-like reach for the summit. As we leveled out, the scene became pastoral, and the trees gave way to grass and ponds. The mountains produced a feeling of power and strength and towered over us in every direction. The valley was all peace and serenity. I had the thought that someone should bring all the crazy people up here and they would all be calmed, probably even be cured.

We left the main road and approached a gateway identifying our destination. We had arrived at Little Green Valley YMCA Camp. Let the fun begin!

⌘

Impressed! That was my reaction. There was a large, rustic-appearing building with a campfire area out in front. All the buses pulled into the clearing there, and all of us young Christians spilled out. I was at camp; so far, so good.

There were a million kids milling around, gathering their sleeping bags and luggage and being herded into groups by alphabetic selection. I headed for the S's, knowing from experience that about a million Smiths would be in line with me. "S" lines were always long. These people were good at organizing kids. Processing was fast and in no time I was on my way to Cabin 5.

Now, for the moment, instead of being one of a million kids, I was one of twelve. The upper bunks were already taken, which was a bit of a disappointment. All boys think the upper is more fun. No big deal. I selected a lower next to the wall, which seemed a bit more remote and private, and privacy was going to be at a premium. For an only child, this was going to be a major departure from my accustomed bedroom singularism. Group living—a new concept—but I had expected to share quarters. It would be okay.

Things slowed down a bit, which gave my bladder an opportunity to send me a message—namely that it had been a long time since I had gone to the bathroom. For the first time I noticed that there was no bathroom in Cabin 5. I would have to inquire as to the location of a restroom.

One of the kids in Cabin 5 was obviously a veteran of Y camp. He knew too much and seemed too comfortable to be as new to the game as I, so I asked him. What he found amusing about the question was a mystery to me, but I kept my cool and waited him out. He advised me that "Bean Alley" could be found simply "by following one's nose," and he was once again amused rather than informative. I gave up on him, since finding a restroom anywhere in America should be little problem, I thought. The situation wasn't really critical, but I would need to know the whereabouts of a toilet sooner or later, so I figured this was as good a time as any.

Up by Cabin 1 was a sign post indicating where everything was located: "Arts & Crafts," "Swimmin' Hole," etc. To my surprise, Bean Alley was indeed listed, with its own arrow. There was no arrow for, or mention of, "restrooms" or "toilets," so Bean Alley must be it.

I had my clue. I headed in the direction designated for Bean Alley as indicated by the arrow. If Bean Alley was where the restrooms were, it was not very convenient. I had walked some distance before a second arrow sign advised me I was on the correct course. It was about then I noticed a change in the air quality. There were a number of boys coming up the trail as I continued, and I was overtaken by a few who were obviously in some crisis and were wasting no time in their quest for a restroom. I, too, was beginning to experience some urgency and quickened my step as well. A serious odor now intensified, obviously originating somewhere in the direction I was headed. This was unpleasant and getting worse. The mountains were not supposed to smell like this, and I made a conscious decision to seek another restroom area next time I needed to go. However, for now I was committed.

I arrived at a large, shedlike structure with a sign in the center which identified it as Bean Alley. It became obvious that Bean Alley was, in fact, the source of the horrendous odor that by now was literally wilting the pine needles on the nearby trees. I wondered how anything could grow here. My eyes and nose were burning, but so was my bladder. I really had to go now.

There were two doors, one on each side of the sign. Kids were going in and kids were coming out. No one was just standing around except me, and I couldn't take much more or the sack lunch I ate on the bus was going to make an unwelcome appearance.

I entered Bean Alley. The stench was so bad, my eyes were watering; it was difficult to focus. When blurry images began to take form, I tried to make sense of what was going on here. Harold had not discussed Bean Alley.

To my amazement, kids were sitting side by side on a board seat with holes cut in it, trousers bunched up around their ankles. They were doing number two! Impossible, I thought. No Christian organization would allow something like this. I was pretty sure this was a sin! No one had invaded the sanctity of my bathroom since I learned to wipe myself and flush. That was a long time ago. I backed out the door barely avoiding a collision with a kid making a hasty entry.

Outside I took my first breath in what seemed like about twenty minutes, and tried to get control of a rising panic attack. Complicating my thought process was severe urinary urgency. This was not going to wait until I could find the *civilized* bathroom. I was going to have to face going back in there.

The smell inside was so bad that the air outside now seemed mountain fresh. I partook in deep gasps, building up courage and stored air to see me through the hastiest urinary process I had ever achieved. It was a success, but in the process I learned a serious lesson. I would never be able to sit down for number two in that place. Even if it weren't so vile, it would still be too primitive and far too public.

✕✕

I was stunned to discover there was no civilized "other" bathroom. Bean Alley was not only *it* as far as bathrooms went, it was somewhat of an institution at Y camp—a kind of ordeal one was expected to endure sans complaint, indeed, with an air of nonchalance and bravado. Achievable perhaps by members of large families or those of very low breeding, but impossible for anyone raised in a dignified atmosphere of bathroom etiquette like myself. Dignity, however, was not going to solve my bowel problem for the next ten days. I would need an idea or a herculean-sized will. The dinner gong was sounding and I pushed Bean Alley from my thoughts. Let's see what the food looks like. Please, God, no onions. I hated onions.

Dinner that first night was no great thrill either. I didn't expect my grandmother's cooking, and it wasn't. It was hearty, but I was used to individual portions cooked to my known taste in food. For one thing, that meant no onions. My grandmother cooked special meals for me without onions.

It takes a great cook to prepare food without onions and make it delicious. My mother and grandmother had become professional at it. The Y camp cooks obviously were not interested in competing with them. Consequently, everything but the milk had onions. My appetite was lost, and I knew my problems with camp adjustment were going to be serious.

It didn't matter what kind of potatoes they served, they all had onions. Fried with onions, mashed with onions, boiled with onions, scalloped with onions. Just as well, I thought. The less I eat, the less I face the indignity of a visit to Bean Alley. But how long could I live on milk and pancakes (what, no onions in the pancakes?) while avoiding a bowel movement? Ten days? Was it possible? My tactics were shaping up. The meat loaf was full of onions, too.

I had one other idea—not very appealing, but perhaps a relief valve if needed. I would remain awake after the others were asleep, take some napkins obtained at dinner and sneak off a distance from camp to do my business. This would be very foreign to my American Standard dependency, but it seemed workable.

Not for long. After dinner we gathered at the campfire to receive our major orientation address, and among other things, we were warned to stay within camp boundaries, especially at night, since bear activity was most prevalent then. Just what I needed—to be attacked and killed by a bear while squatting in the woods. No thanks. Scratch that idea.

❧

I stared into the flames of the campfire and pictured the kids of Pacific Lane, especially Harold. Right now I needed Harold! He was a more creative thinker than I and would surely have a solution to my problem with Bean Alley and the onion-dominated menu.

I thought about the lockable door on our bathroom and wondered how I could convince time to go more swiftly. Why, I wondered, wasn't camp just one week? Who would knowingly volunteer for an eternity-like ten days of Bean Alley? Everyone was singing but me. My eyes were burning and my throat felt like something too big was stuck in it. Day one was ending on a note of impending doom. Alone, I headed for Cabin 5.

❧

The zipper on my sleeping bag wouldn't work, and a mountain breeze outside Cabin 5 became a cooling breeze inside, revealing my choice of bunks to be a poor one. The more I attempted to wrap the zipper side around and under me, the more entangled I became and the more lumps I created. Everyone else seemed to be sleeping, breathing deeply and occasionally calling out to someone undistinguishable, undoubtedly a parent. Still, at least they were asleep. I couldn't get warm enough.

The recording of taps had sounded over the public address system hours ago, it seemed, but I was as wide awake as I had been the previous night, contemplating my departure to camp—alone! Tomorrow, I had learned at campfire, I would begin the compulsory quest for my "purple rag," a neckerchief which would identify me as a one-year veteran of Y Camp, and, I thought, a survivor of Bean Alley. Whatever the two-year rag color was, no one would ever see me with one on; that was a given. If I lived through this, I would never return to this torture camp.

The instant I fell asleep, the bugle sounded reveille, and Cabin 5 sprang to life—at least eleven of the twelve young Christians—and eagerly dressed for breakfast. I was number twelve and could see no particular reason to rush over to "onion city." I had this vision of onion oatmeal. No thanks!

The breakfasts were okay, as it turned out. There were no onions in the pancakes or cereal, so it looked like I would, as I had hoped, have one meal a day to sustain me.

The central question that was forming was this: Could a human survive ten days without a bowel movement? The answer, I decided, was yes, but only if necessary to avoid Bean Alley. I was prepared to enter that ghastly chamber of horrors for urinary purposes, but only when my bladder was ready to burst and for as long as I could hold my breath.

Things were a lot more regimented than I cared for. I was accustomed to a much more democratic system at home, and lining up for meals, eating at a particular table by the numbers, compulsory participation in activities, and "ragger" duties were not very attractive to me. My attitude did not provide me with an identity as a "fun guy," and consequently I was not making friends. The other kids seemed to be having fun. I was not making any leather wallets or key chains. I was just wandering around waiting for time to pass and trying not to think about my stomach.

We were expected to learn the twenty-third psalm and the words to a Y camp song. The psalm part alluding to "the valley of the shadow of death" was beginning to take on special meaning to me, because after just a few days of pancakes and milk going in with nothing going out, I was quickly losing my former healthy appearance.

My eyes appeared to be sinking inward, as if being pulled by the weight building up inside and below. I was becoming a living, walking, talking Hefty bag full of toxic waste. If I had been dropped on Berlin, I probably would have ended the war. My complexion was a lot like pancake batter.

With about five days to go, I started feeling really bad. The small amount of pancakes I could get down wouldn't stay down. Surprise, surprise. No more room in the Hefty bag! The pile of toxic waste seemed to be piled up to a point just below my Adam's apple.

I was not good at vomiting then, and I'm still not. It scares the hell out of me. I lose my breath, gag, choke, get tears in my eyes, the sour stuff comes up and out of my nose as well as my mouth, and I really expect to die. I was just too young then for my life to pass before my eyes.

But vomiting was becoming routine and was soon replaced by an even more terrifying syndrome called "dry heaves." In other words, I kept throwing up—nothing! Rather than relieving the situation like regular heaving tends to do, dry heaves seem to perpetuate the condition from dry to even drier.

What all this vomiting meant was that my intestines and all the space around them were full of pancakes. They were determined to come out but they were beyond the point of no return. There was only one way out and that was effectively blocked by Bean Alley and my overworked sphincter muscles.

At this point my counselor began to be concerned. It was time, he decided, to alert the camp big shot that I might need some medical attention. I was barfing most of the time and I was not looking well.

The big shot's name was Ted. He was barrel chested and the most macho Christian the YMCA ever spawned. One look told me Ted did not like sick kids. He liked kids who aspired to be the best ragger a ragger could be. One look told him I was not a kid he would be snapping a towel at over at the "Old Swimmin' Hole"—not ever! I was pathetic. But my eyes told Ted something was wrong here, and when I launched into a series of the dreaded dry heaves, Ted sent down the hill for a doctor—(what, they didn't even have a doctor in camp? Nope!)—and this only produced more anxiety. What, I wondered, would the doctor discover? If it was revealed that I could not face the ordeal of Bean Alley, Ted was certain to expose me at camp-fire as an example of a sissy kid who should never be sent to Y camp. He might make me sit in Bean Alley for the remainder of the week, breathing fumes that would melt my lungs and award me a "pink rag"—probably posthumously.

Perhaps the doctor would elect to operate on the spot. I could only imagine what would happen when the scalpel released the com-pacted contents straining within my distended, rock-hard abdomen. Would the stuff look like chewed up pancakes or the stuff that falls into the toilet—perhaps something in between?

I decided to admit nothing. After all, he was a doctor. Let him figure out what was wrong. What I really wanted to do was be ex-cused from the ragger ceremony for medical reasons. I didn't fear death anymore. With two days to go, I knew I could make it—dry heaves or no.

Perhaps the doctor would order me to be delivered home by spe-cial car, to live out my final few days. Maybe I *was* dying after all. In any case, no ragger ceremony for me. I didn't know the Y camp song or the twenty-third Psalm.

The doctor arrived, looked me over, looked in my eyes, listened to my heart and watched me dry heave. He then announced his diag-nosis, which served to frame my opinion of doctors forever. "This kid," he told Ted, "has a classic and severe case of *homesickness!*" What a jerk, I thought, but the diagnosis sounded like a special car home, so who cared if he was a jerk?

But the doctor continued, "No one dies of homesickness. Get him involved. That's the best medicine. Don't pamper him."

Just what Ted, the chest without a brain, wanted to hear. I started dry heaving, but Ted eased me out of Cabin 5 and into the sunshine. I was headed for a session of singing and psalming, last-minute preparations for tomorrow's ceremony. I still didn't know the stuff, but tomorrow was the final day. I would have to fake it.

We gathered at the campfire area and formed a circle around it. It was time to sing and recite. As the counselors came within range to verify my knowledge of the ragger-required oratory, I would pro-duce a dry heave that would move them along without a pause.

"Yea (urp) though I walk (urp) through the (gag, urp) valley of death"—and soon it was over. I was presented with my purple rag and promptly urped in it.

There was no pity in the eyes of the others anymore. They looked at me with disgust. Word had gotten around that I wasn't sick at all—just homesick! Ted had leaked the diagnosis to the camp grapevine. His hatred had become overt, and he was determined to turn the entire camp population against me. So what? I would be going home tomorrow and Little Green Valley, Bean Alley, poison onions, and Ted would all seem like a bad dream from the distant past as I exploded into my own home toilet.

To some degree the doctor must have been right, because my dry heaves were not nearly as severe, owing, I must assume, to the fact that home seemed closer than it had a few days ago. I was not a healthy kid, however.

Ted and company couldn't wait to get me on the bus. I had seat number one, window! I could have demanded about anything and Ted would have acquiesced. There were no demands since I just wanted home and a ceramic pot to sit down on—in private!

During the trip home I didn't feel good, but I was so glad to be going home that it *seemed* like I felt good. I was in the minority. Most of the kids had loved Y camp and were not crazy to go home at all. Too bad. A few more days and I would have exploded, creating a really awful mess all over everybody.

Down the hill we went in our purple rag neckerchiefs, me included. I didn't drink in the scenery as I had on the way up to camp. My needs had changed too drastically. The glorious reality was that every mile put me closer to home and further away from Bean Alley.

My parents had been advised that I wasn't feeling so good, but my mother was not prepared for my appearance. At this point I would rather have played my condition down. Sympathy was not my basic need, not at all. In fact, I really didn't want to confess the source of my near-terminal condition. I was not proud of myself.

The problem was, I couldn't downplay this thing because I could no longer stand up straight. My impacted intestines had assumed the contour of the bus seat and wouldn't straighten out. The pancakes had become cement. I was bent over at a right angle and my mother was aghast. She wanted to find someone for my dad to pound into oatmeal. It wouldn't require much coaxing; my dad would have made quick work of Ted. But there was no time for that. I convinced my mother that what I needed was not revenge; I needed a session in the bathroom. The problem, I told her, was that I was constipated and hadn't been able to get any relief at camp. Now, I told her, I had the urge and needed to hastily take advantage of the moment. "We need to get home," I urged.

It wasn't really a lie. In fact it was fairly accurate, and she was convinced. We were homeward bound, Mom, Dad, Lucky, and I. Things would be okay now.

🔀

School would be starting soon. I had wasted two prime weeks of precious—no, priceless—summer vacation. I loved both—I loved summer and I loved vacation—and I didn't intend to waste one more minute. Just being home was a good start at salvaging my precious summer. Mom was grateful to see me standing up straight again, and my grandmother was thrilled about my appetite, which had been dormant, waiting for some room to be created down in the digestive territory. "No pancakes, Grandma. Cereal will be just fine for breakfast." Pancakes—gag, urp!

🔀

Being nine years old means possessing an ability to survive and recover quickly from situations that would be fatal for an adult. In no time I was good as new—ready for whatever fun Harold, Boo, and all the Pacific Lane kids had stored up in my absence. I attacked the subject of play with a new energy that surprised even Harold, who held the record for play at the nine-year-old level.

Jovine was running around with no shirt or blouse or whatever, and her nipples were noticeably bigger than Harold's, Boo's, or mine. They were kind of interesting, and I tried to study the difference without alarming Jovine into doing something I might regret, like covering herself just as I was discovering one of life's new mysterious frontiers. Thanks to the warmth of glorious summer, Jovine's nipples were on display for my insouciant "see me not looking at your nipples" performance. Another gift of the glorious summer season.

But life's lessons are hard, and I was facing my last summer without that beautiful bike. My birthday was in January. I loved summer, but I needed winter.

Harold and Boo had delivered and sold my magazines. My dad had helped out to see that things went okay and my "regulars" were taken care of. Selling magazines was about the only thing I didn't miss during my Y camp ordeal, but compared to a session at Bean Alley, selling magazines was a walk in the park.

I hadn't seen a comic book for two weeks, and who was waiting for me but Sheena, the queen of my jungle, in a new adventure with Bill. I wondered, as I studied Sheena's anatomy, if Jovine's chest would one day look like that. Was Jovine a nine-year-old potential Sheena? I would spend considerable time developing that idea—secretly, of course, *very secretly*.

⚎

This time Harold had found a half dollar! It was not a rare coin in 1941, but it was sure rare to *find* one. Leave it to the human metal detector.

Harold and I had discussed on a number of occasions just what heaven would be like. He thought it would consist of unlimited Three Musketeers candy bars; I leaned toward Powerhouse. While it was true we had a sweet tooth bonanza at Howdy's, the fare consisted of fountain treats. Neither of us had a nickel candy bar to himself very often.

The magnitude of Harold's find made him generous. We headed for Colburn's Market and a candy counter with mountains of candy. Harold quite naturally bought five Three Musketeers—five Powerhouses for me. We were about to experience pleasure beyond our wildest dreams, a feast fit for a couple of kid kings.

The first two bars went down tasting as I expected, but as I unwrapped the third, I realized I had overestimated my Powerhouse capability. These were really *big* candy bars and this third one really didn't look all that good to me.

Harold was on his third but slowing considerably as I bit into my number three. A second bite was the limit; I had hit the wall. Harold finished number three but had no intention of opening number four.

Now a feeling of guilt came over us. We didn't feel we could take the remaining candy home because we didn't want to admit that we had spent an entire half dollar on candy. The foolishness of the act now hit us. We anticipated a serious inquisition and we didn't want that. To tell my dad that I had spent an entire quarter on candy was never going to happen! Anna just might consider cutting us off at the soda fountain, too.

We just didn't see any options. We loved this candy and would surely be disappointed in ourselves later on if we just wasted it— threw it away or gave it away. There was no way out. We had to eat the rest of the candy.

The short "time out" had provided us with the feeling that we could duplicate our earlier effort. I would have to do a bit more. Harold only had two more to go. We were motivated, but our resolve wilted quickly only a few bites into the program. How could the candy have tasted so good an hour ago? From ecstasy to agony in only sixty minutes. Harold did not look too good. He was fighting a psychological problem. Although Three Musketeers was smaller than Powerhouse, it came in three pieces and seemed like three candy bars. His gameness was being prominently displayed though. Harold was going to make it, and I was unwrapping number four.

We both made it. We ate five candy bars each, and when I say we both ate the *last* one, I mean the last one *forever*! It took us beyond those name brands. We never really thought of candy the same way again. Maybe we even understood a little bit about Anna's rationing techniques at Howdy's. It would be terrible to hate her fabulous thick chocolate malts. We had learned a valuable lesson about too much of a good thing.

Postscript: I have never in my life met another human being who ate five Powerhouse candy bars at one time.

❌

A terrible war was raging in Europe. We were hearing of the bravery of the English and Russians who were resisting the maniac Hitler and his buffoon-like Italian henchman, Mussolini. America was sending lots of weapons to aid the resistance, so everyone was working now and things looked rosy on the surface, but the way the war was spreading had the adult population very nervous.

We kids, however, enjoyed a typical Fourth of July. Fireworks were, of course, legal and inexpensive. We blew up tin cans with fire-crackers, put them in red ant hills, risking the curse of the devil ants, and lit whole packages at a time. It was a great holiday. We built flying model planes for the specific purpose of blowing them up with a firecracker. All kinds of damaged toys were earmarked for destruc-tion—and an occasional mailbox was victimized. Pets were safe but kept indoors because the noise terrified them. There were never-ending arguments over which brand of firecracker was the most pow-erful—Red Devil or Black Panther.

Everybody had heard about a kid who had blown off a finger or two but we never really seemed to meet one personally. In fact, al-most every kid had experienced a quick fuse and burned fingers numbed by the exploding firecracker, but fingers remained in place as far as my experience and that of my mates was concerned. The fuses were very unpredictable. Sometimes they burned so slowly that the explosion came only after one had given up and decided to exam-ine the reason for failure. Then in a split second, the fuse would flare up and the cracker would explode before one could get clear. Others would explode literally as the fuse was ignited. There was only a frac-tion of a second to sense the need to be rid of it. I only tell this in de-tail because this holiday provided kid pleasure second only to Christ-mas—and it has vanished. The holiday stolen by the fire department overreacting to the fire dangers attributed to fireworks. The Fourth of July is gone and no '40s-era kids would agree with a fire marshal that the planned fireworks displays today are a better way to go. An-other major piece of Americana lost without a whimper, and the irony is the Fourth is *symbolic* of America; at least it used to be. It exists no more, not the *real* Fourth of July.

Lucky stayed inside—not as terrified as most dogs, but not pleased about all the noise either. She would curl up under the kitchen range (they were up on legs then) and wait for the craziness to end. We kids wanted it to last forever. It was the next best thing to Christmas, lasting from early morning to midnight.

It was a favorite picnic and reunion day, adding to the scope of the holiday. The public parks were jammed with people. Beer, watermelon, fried chicken, and hot dogs were part and parcel of an overall event called "the Fourth of July." We never called it "Independence Day." Patriotism swelled in everyone's breast, and the red-white-and-blue of flags and bunting were ubiquitous. Bands played Sousa marches and every politician in America at every level fought for rostrum time. Every town had a parade. Was it perhaps even *better* than Christmas?

Harold, Boo, Richard, and I packed as much of it into our day as we could. Comic books, sports, malts, Jovine's nipples, all would wait while we were in town for the parade, at the parks, everywhere the action was. Armed with our firecrackers we added to the action wherever we went. The mood was very festive, so even if we managed to startle someone, it was accepted good naturedly. It was part of the idea behind firecrackers. Summer vacation really was heaven on earth!

✠

For Californians there was a summer bonus: the beach! While my parents were not as enthusiastic as I, some family in the neighborhood would always be going and would be willing to include another kid or two. It was a step beyond for me; I could never get enough. How could someone born in Nebraska have sea water in his veins? I did. I still do, and I always will. The only thing that kept me from getting to the beach on my own was a bike. Just wait for the summer of '42, I told myself.

Adding to my beach pleasure was the fact that I was a good swimmer—no fear of the water, but a healthy respect for it. My dad had taught me to swim in a Nebraska lake. He and a friend pushed me back and forth a few times and I was swimming. It was pretty natural, thanks to the trouble they went to. They made it fun, so I swam.

If you loved the ocean, had a fascination for it like I did, you would soon be drawn to body surfing like I was. In the '40s there were few board surfers. Surfboards were large, heavy, and awkward. The name of the game was body surfing. Somehow the participants would convince a wave to deliver them, sometimes a quarter of a mile, to the beach, often right at the feet of admiring girls or less adventuresome bathers.

Getting used to the ocean is done in stages. Most people don't swim in the ocean; they stand in it. The waves either crash into them, or if the bathers venture a bit deeper, each wave lifts and gently deposits them in place as it continues its journey to the shore. It is a pleasant, weightless feeling. Some, however, get much more from the sea. They would be the body surfers.

To me, body surfers were like men who had learned the secrets of the fish—mastery of the ocean—human dolphins at play in their element. Sheer poetry. Body surfing didn't look easy to me, so I didn't just plunge in and try it. I watched. I watched from the beach and then, sometime later, I swam out beyond the breakers, out where they were, and watched some more. I didn't want to drown before I had at least a few successes.

The trick was to position oneself at precisely the right spot, to be able to feel the wave accept you as it began to crest, and to recognize if the wave was "right"—the right size and the right configuration. Then the physical part began. One had to outswim the wave as it gathered momentum for "the break."

Once one "had" the wave, the next trick was to keep it. That part is hard to discover through observation; the technique is hidden, the secret of the sea and the man-fish. To learn, one must ask a surfer or discover the secret by accident, trial and error.

The surfer I asked considered it no secret at all. He shared his knowledge willingly, and I began to body surf, or attempt it, anyway.

Knowing the secret was not enough. I had to learn to swim a bit better and faster. Like most accomplishments, it required practice, patience, and some pain—pain because there were other secrets, and only the ocean knew them all.

Some waves had "too much water," a seeming oxymoron, but it simply meant the wave had the wrong configuration to crest properly and would not provide proper impetus to propel the surfer. There was no danger in this. One would simply be left swimming with no wave and probably miss "the perfect wave."

The danger and the pain came with the failure to recognize the "pounder"—the wave that would take you down and under instead of gliding you to the shore. Again, it is a matter of the surfer sensing the wave's intent. All body surfers have been pounder victims and will be again.

My lesson came early and violently. The pounder took me straight down—how deep I have no idea—and drove my head into the sandy bottom with great force. How did I escape a broken neck? I have no idea. I was then bounced, head over heels, totally out of control, scraped on the bottom, where I left some skin, lifted and dropped, and finally, when I thought my breath was exhausted and I would gasp and drown, I was deposited on the shore, dazed and disoriented. When my thoughts began to gather, I realized I had an audience—an amused audience.

I was sitting upright as the pounder had arranged me, feet pointed shoreward. My bathing suit I realized had received special attention by the pounder to underscore the lesson; it was saturated with sand and rolled tightly around my ankles! The reason, undoubtedly, for the amused, gathering crowd.

I began a futile struggle to unravel the suit and pull it up where it belonged. It was hopeless. Then the logical solution occurred to me. Instead of pulling the suit up, I pulled the suit *off!* I walked waist deep into the surf and unrolled the suit and put it on, this time with some attention to the drawstring. The audience was dispersing and I received some applause.

I surprised myself by not really feeling very embarrassed. I was going to be a body surfer, and we body surfers were usually nearly nude anyway—and we were cool! I was more concerned about recognizing the "pounder" next time around. I slipped under a breaker and headed confidently out to catch me a wave.

ⅠⅩⅠ

Vacation was flying by, although I wasn't watching the calendar. Someone would tell me in plenty of time that school was starting up again. I wasn't too upset about school. There were lots of friends I hadn't seen and looked forward to being with again. I just hated to see summer end. How sweet it was.

We were all tan as berries and the warm sun and the free-flowing appearance of my pals seduced me into experimenting with barefootedness once again, but the episode ended as usual—I cut my foot again. My dad said he figured I would never learn, but I really envied my leather-footed pals, and it was worth the risk two or three times a summer. To be unshod in California in the summertime seemed the natural way to be. Mother Nature considered me a Nebraska kid misplaced in California, and used my feet to remind me about three times every season.

Summer was winding down. I knew this would be Jovine's last topless season, and I had this gnawing feeling that my interest would be increasing as my opportunity to observe would be decreasing proportionately. Life really was funny.

I decided to broach the subject of Jovine's nipples to Harold to see if they generated any peculiar feelings in him. I just couldn't seem to recognize what it was that piqued my curiosity so.

The probe was unproductive. Harold thought of all girls as potential Glorias, and that made the subject purely unpleasant. All I learned was that Gloria's nipples were larger than Jovine's, even. Hmm. More food for thought. Boo's sister Daisy was older than Gloria, and her chest looked a lot more like Sheena's. Perhaps some well-rehearsed questions directed at Boo would be productive. Hmm.

Summer continued to flash by—golden days of games, the beach, Howdy's, Saturday matinee serials, not to mention Abbott and Costello and Red Skelton movies. The Grand Theater was aptly named.

✶

We had some friends just outside town, former Nebraskans, who were farming, raising some crops and maintaining a small dairy herd. A family of five—all with orange-red hair and millions of freckles. They were the Cheesicks.

It was fun to go with my dad to visit. It seemed like there were one or two of every farm animal I had ever heard of. Upon arrival, Lucky would dash from the car and be in the barn before an eye could blink. A rat terrier at work. She never ate mice and rats; she just killed them. A genetic phenomenon on display, she was awesome.

Mr. Cheesick was impressed. Lucky paid no attention to other animals. She was of a singular mind, dedicated to one purpose—the elimination of vermin.

Mr. Cheesick's own dog almost always had a dead chicken tied to its collar—a sure cure for chicken killers that never worked. The dog seemed pitiful and confused. I really felt sorry for him. I was surprised that Mr. Cheesick didn't shoot him, and as bad as I felt for the poor miserable dog, I didn't know if I wished him dead or not. Always having a dead chicken tied to his neck didn't seem like much of a life to me.

The Cheesicks were wonderful people, and I sometimes stayed overnight. Boy, girl, boy was the order of the kids: Duane (Red), Polly, and Jerry. Red was a year older than I and got the nickname only because he was born first. Polly was my age, and Jerry a year younger. They were all outgoing, friendly people. They loved each other, and when I stayed, one would have thought I had red hair, too. I was accepted and treated as one of the family. That's the way they were. None of the kids had Ronnie Kronk's explosive temperament. Red hair must not be the cause.

For some reason the food Mrs. Cheesick cooked tasted wonderful to me even though I probably would have refused to touch it at home. For example, sauerkraut and pig tails! Yes, not something *called* pig tails, actual pig's tails. I can taste that food now as I close my eyes and think of it.

For some reason I fit in—an only child in a family of five. I loved them all and felt a sense of belonging. I was surely one of a dozen unborn Reds they had emotional room for, so instead of being a visitor, I was more like a visiting son.

The Cheesicks had a horse and Red could ride like Hopalong Cassidy. He familiarized me with the animal and I was soon comfortable in the saddle. The horse was very gentle and as friendly as his owners. So a small-town, citified boy got a bit of the country infused in him—just enough to know what it was about so he could properly appreciate that side of life. Lucky stayed over as well, and she became a farm dog, sleeping beside her farm boy.

The Cheesicks lived a hard life with few luxuries, but it was evident that luxuries were not what they sought. They sought to be themselves, without any pretense, and material things seemed to add nothing to their lives. They only sought the things that were required to continue their lifestyle—required rather than coveted things.

The Cheesicks' farm was another classroom, an institution of the highest learning for me. Not everyone, I learned, lived for money, new cars, and luxurious houses. Some people lived for each other and the wonderful things that life offers, the rewards of being on one's own—independent, planting things, breeding things, and growing things that are real and necessary to life.

The Cheesicks obtained another horse, which surprised me because since tractors became available and affordable, horses no longer contributed much to farming. In fact, they were excess baggage except to farm kids and farm dads. They were really just big pets. The addition of the little pinto was sure great for me, though, because Red liked having riding companionship, and I was eager to ride more, and I exhibited some aptitude for it.

Riding horses made me forget a bit about the bike. I knew I would one day have a bike, but I sensed that my equestrian days were surely numbered. Unfortunately my intuition was to prove all too accurate, but for now summer vacation was sure looking like a record setter. Y camp was fading into the past as I became the rare city kid who had horse sense in the literal way.

Red would come over to my house on his little filly, with the Pinto in tow. The kids would congregate and we would give favored pals a little ride before Red and I went off together. I was learning to ride, but it would take a lot of riding to be as good as Red. I didn't expect that to happen. Red had a big head start and he owned the horses, plus one could see that Red and his horses were on a wavelength; they understood one another, they communicated. The problem was the pinto had a mean streak, and she was bigger and stronger than the kid on her back.

I love horses, but I am not a "horse lover." That's a noun and the title belongs to a special genre of people. Horse lovers will not appreciate it when I say that horses are really not very smart. In fact, most farmers will tell you that among farm animals, horses are really pretty dumb.

However, they are, I learned, smart enough to know if they want someone on their backs or not, even though the one astride them is most often their best friend and, moreover, the only friend they have. They are often not smart enough to know that. Red's little pinto, Patches, never figured it out.

Horses have weapons; their kick can be lethal, and their bite un-expected and painful. When they buck you can find yourself flying through the air, completely out of control with no way to soften the impact—a very helpless and frightening position to be in—poten-tially lethal. Yet another method is for the animal to try to scrape the rider from its back using a low branch or something of that nature, and finally they might use their weight to purposely injure a rider.

One day after Red and I had galloped through a hobo camp out-side of town (a harmless prank that surprised the transient residents but had no potential to harm or do damage), kicking up a lot of dust which resulted in a few shouted threats that were never heard or meant, Patches caught Red's leg between her body and a tree trunk. It only took a second, but the great weight of the horse, the unyielding nature of the tree, and the flesh-and-blood fragility of Red's leg made it no contest. Red cried out, then swore, then slapped Patches on the neck and swore some more. He dismounted and I was relieved to see him able to walk. That should mean his leg wasn't broken; anyway, that's what I had heard.

Red pulled his pant leg up and found the leg to be pretty badly bruised. Red's skin was so white a bruise was as noticeable as if ink had been spilled on him. Surrounding the bruise was a zone of angry red flesh. It hurt plenty and I was getting another lesson. No tears from Red; his anger transcended his pain. He was really tough, was what I thought.

By the time Red got home that day, his knee was badly swollen. Such injuries on the Cheesick farm would get you sympathy and some home treatment, but there would be no dash to a doctor's of-fice. Nobody was dying.

Soon, however, it became clear that the knee was full of fluid that just was not going to go away. In fact, it was getting worse and signs of infection appeared.

It was touch and go for a while. Red's leg was dangerously near amputation before his youth and health and will overpowered the in-fection; there were no wonder drugs. However, Red was a growing boy and his uninjured leg grew a couple of inches in length before the injured one got started again.

This event soured me on riding. Red couldn't ride for quite a while, but I didn't ride a horse again for a long time—not because I was afraid, I just felt so bad for Red that I didn't like horses very much for a long time.

Red and I lost touch for many years, and when we met again at long last, I surprised Red when I described my feelings about horses after his accident; he surprised me even more when he told me that he was a race horse trainer and had been in a saddle virtually every day since our lives had pulled us in different directions. It really made me happy to know that Red had recovered and that he had dealt with the effects of his injury successfully, but I still don't ride horses.

⚎

The Germans were on a roll and all of us democracy-loving, red-blooded Americans were not happy about it. Hitler and his Nazis with their Stuka dive bombers, Panzer tanks, Gestapo—it all seemed so sinister, so evil. One wondered how such evil could exist in such numbers. How could God allow them to be so successful? The lurking U-boat submarines ruled the Atlantic Ocean and sank ships at will, leaving oil-soaked sailors bobbing like tiny black corks on a vast, hostile ocean of hopelessness. The enemy seemed so cruel.

All kids worshipped heroes and imagined themselves as heroes. Winston Churchill was a hero. All the English people were heroes, but the kind of heroes we wanted to be were the daring type. R.A.F. pilots were that kind. Commandos were that kind too. We spent a lot of time thinking about heroes like them. Their numbers were soon to grow, and they wouldn't be restricted to the English. A world disaster was unfolding rapidly, but for the kids of Pacific Lane, these were exciting times.

There were stories of Americans in the war, and the idea thrilled us. A group of fliers was in China fighting the Japanese. They called themselves the "Flying Tigers" and their P-40 fighter planes were painted with sharks' mouths to make them look frightening. They looked wonderful to us. We were told they actually did frighten the

Japanese pilots, but in reality it was for the psyche of the American pilots. In that respect, it worked. They were fantastically effective. How we kids adored them as they screamed through the sky, shooting down the invading, cruel Japanese.

The U.S. was sending lots of planes and tanks to the English and Russians. America was in the process of gearing up to produce goods for a war effort that would establish the country as *the* world power, but it would take everything and then some to get the job done. We kids felt cheated—too young to do anything but be spectators, but we were prepared to make the very best of it. We didn't realize how lucky our age group really was. The war was a world away.

Summer came to an end and school started up. Our emotions were mixed as the freedom of summer vacation was replaced by the renewed friendships of classmates not seen for some three months— or was it three minutes—or three years? The passage of time was mysterious in the effect it had on us. Everyone had grown a bit, especially, it seemed, the girls. Subtle differences were taking place. The sexes were somehow a bit more distanced from each other—not in a hostile way but in a way that seemed to make everyone uncomfortable. We had all grown up just a tiny bit, into our future, the part that we never grow up enough to totally understand. The girls began to leave us behind in the race to maturity—a race we hadn't willingly entered and were not prepared to participate in.

Chizuko and Sakio were back. They seemed a little older too, which kept them a bit ahead of the rest of us, as usual. They were reserved but friendly—dignified, not aloof. They played no role; they were just two nice girls—Japanese-American girls.

1941 was winding down, and in typical fashion, people were thinking about Christmas when the Japanese attacked Pearl Harbor. This was an event of such magnitude that even kids eight, nine, and ten years of age had a perfunctory understanding of what had happened. We had a new, mysterious enemy.

President Roosevelt explained it in pretty understandable terms, and although not many kids knew the relationship of Hawaii to the U.S., or had even heard of Pearl Harbor, we sure understood "dastardly" and "sneak attack" and "infamy."

We had some early problems with the size of Japan, which seemed a bit like the flea vs. the elephant in our estimation. We thought they had to be fools.

Adults and kids alike failed to interpret the depth of the wound that the sneak attack had inflicted, and for propaganda purposes, and even more for tactical purposes, minimization of that aspect of the event was orchestrated perfectly—serious enough to be an unspeakable, cowardly outrage, but not so serious as to demoralize or alter a certain, swift, and lethal reaction from the great, honorable, and "godly" United States of America. They would soon be sorry was the way we assessed the situation.

The Japanese, we reasoned, could not shoot straight for obvious reasons. Rumors leaked out information that the "zero" fighter plane was superior to our on-line fighters, but they were rejected by most people, not just by kids. It was quite true, and in the early going the Japanese pilots feasted on Brewster Buffalo, Grumman Wildcat, and P-40 Kittyhawk, never a well-known fact but painfully true.

America flew into action with the resolve some visionary Japanese "warlords" feared. Indeed the tail of the tiger had been tweaked, and Japan's ultimate defeat was sealed. America really didn't know its own strength. Victory, however, lay many difficult and perilous months and years ahead, but for the kid population, the adventure now included us in a real sense. England had seemed so far away. We had our own war now, and patriotism obscured the serious reality of the situation. It was really exciting.

✹

Every few days I made a visit to Western Auto to pet my future bike. I never sat on it; it was like we weren't married yet, it wouldn't be right.

I had this sinking feeling that when I had achieved my end of the bike agreement (*if* I achieved my end) I would still be expected to sell magazines. Was I to be a magazine salesman forever? Not a very attractive career, in my estimation. I had really bad dreams about *La-*

dies' Home Journal, like a dead chicken tied around my neck.

I knew full well that once I asked for or agreed to something—anything—once I was involved, my dad expected "commitment." The path leading out was very difficult on purpose! It was like trying to get the Pope to sign your divorce papers—harder even. Simple math indicated at this point that I would successfully earn the required contribution for the birthday bike—that blue-and-silver beauty. My own new Western Flyer, the one with the pet marks all over it.

But I was stressed because of *Ladies' Home Journal.* I needed a life without *Ladies' Home Journal.* Quarter magazines were a trial for a ten-year-old (almost) salesman, regardless of the incentive.

✺

The war had upstaged Christmas—no mean feat in the U.S.—but swarming Japanese soldiers in the Pacific seemed to be endlessly numerous, while in Europe the Germans presented a much different face: a juggernaut, a dark force relentlessly marching forward over a helpless Europe.

It was a very difficult psychological dilemma we kids were dealing with. We wanted America to be invincible, to make duck soup out of these comparatively small countries, but the struggle was colossal. In fact, if one did not know better, one might believe we were actually losing. No, we kids weren't about to believe that!

We found the security blanket we needed. We concluded that the Axis forces drew strength from the depth of their evil, and that we were locked in the ultimate battle between the greatest forces of good vs. the greatest forces of evil. Now we could deal with the setbacks, the apparent defeats. It was just a matter of time until godliness and goodliness prevailed—our side, of course.

The time between December 7 and December 25 was flashing by. With the excitement of the war to distract us, the normal pre-Christmas period, usually torturously slow, literally ambushed us.

From the time I ceased to believe in Santa Claus, my family had celebrated Christmas on Christmas Eve—traditional dinner followed by the opening of gifts. How this all got started or why, we never quite could recall. My parents were not the sleep-in types, so it couldn't be explained that way.

The dinner was a carbon copy of Thanksgiving dinner: turkey and all the trimmings, cooked to perfection by my mother and grandmother, two incomparable professional domestic American cooks. If anyone thinks it was too soon after Thanksgiving to appreciate the duplication, they never tasted food like this. Otherworldly!

This year was different than other years. I had no reason to hurry everyone through dinner. There was nothing I really wanted waiting under the tree. My heart's great desire remained a month distant, the birthday bike, my silver-and-blue Western Flyer.

So I lingered over pumpkin pie with whipped cream. For seconds I would have to choose between raisin (my dad's favorite), chocolate, and apple. The ladies were picking up and dealing with the colossal mess created by such a feast, while my dad grabbed a quick nap prior to the gift giving.

This identical scene was taking place in countless homes in America, a country at war too recently to change old habits. The changes were underway, however. They just hadn't reached the interiors of America's homes as yet—not on Christmas Eve 1941, at any rate.

It took time to do all those dishes in pre-dishwasher America, and drying dishes was one of my chores weekdays, weekends, and holidays, so I reported for duty and we moved efficiently through the restoration of the kitchen. It was a classic example of how to get a job done and make it seem almost pleasant—the "whistle while you work" approach. We were all in a festive mood, overfed and ready for our Christmas, my mother and I singing carols as we worked.

Finally the last glass was in the cupboard, the final fork in the drawer. It was time to gather around the tree and the packages under and around it. There would be mostly clothes for me, and although I had given no real hints regarding my longings, I suspected a baseball glove might be among the precisely wrapped packages. That would be nice.

My grandmother would give me "a nice handkerchief." She gave everyone "a nice handkerchief." I had one for her, too.

Everyone somehow migrated to the living room before me—a bit odd. I usually got there first and waited impatiently for the others. My grandmother would arrive last, a kind of concession to the status her age entitled her to. She was deserving, virtuous in every respect, and we all loved her dearly. Tonight, however, she was already in her place.

As I entered the room, I had that unexplainable sense of multiple eyes intently watching me—and sure enough, they were.

Suddenly, the sun, the moon, and the stars filled the room with a light of such brilliance I was almost blinded. They filled my eyes with hot tears. Could I stand to hold my gaze on the source? Other eyes in that room had responded similarly, but I didn't notice. I was trying to make some sense of what I was seeing.

A bicycle! Right there in the living room stood a brand-new bike. I couldn't believe it. Adding to my astonishment was the fact that this was not the mid-line bike I had saved, hoped, dreamed to one day own; this was the unattainable, impossible dream bike—the top-of-the-line bike. Could I live? Would my heart explode? Did I dare touch it? Was this a dream?

The tears wouldn't stay in my eyes. It was too much. They spilled down my cheeks. The bike wasn't just radiating light, it was radiating love. The moment was as great for my parents and grandmother as it was for me. My reaction was the quid pro quo for all the sacrifice to afford the expensive gift. As they watched me stroke the bike and then look at them, they knew I loved the bike, but it was unmistakable that I loved them more. A bicycle had created a magical moment none of us would ever forget: thoughtfulness, generosity, and gratitude—the recipe for an unforgettable Christmas for a ten-year-old—almost.

✄

The bike was the major Christmas gift among Pacific Lane kid society that year, but getting a lot of envious looks and comments was not that easy. A new bike rather than a used one was a serious qualifier, but it had to be remembered that most kids had a bike of some fashion, so I lost some points in that respect. It was more like I "finally" got one. Of course, to me, that wasn't the central point. I had my bike and I was in heaven. What others thought was of very little importance.

Lucky followed me as I pumped around the neighborhood, but there was a limit. As I ranged further from her familiar territory, she preferred to await my return, which she quickly learned would not be long, else she probably would have suffered the trailing role to exhaustion.

I was working hard, rehearsing in my mind the subject of retirement from magazine sales. After all, I had achieved the desired end; the means were no longer required. I would not rush into a confrontation on this subject. If I was unprepared, I would lose for certain. Even with preparation I lacked confidence regarding the outcome. There was no doubt in my mind that my father liked the idea of my learning responsibility and earning my own way. This sell would be harder than selling *Ladies' Home Journal.*

🔀

Christmas vacation ended, and the bike remained at home with Lucky—both of whom I wished could be with me, but for different reasons neither was appropriate at school. My bike was too new and attracted too much attention. It was safer at home. The separation was agony, but I didn't want a scratch on that beauty, and I sure didn't want it missing. Even then a bike theft was not rare.

🔀

When my tenth birthday rolled around, my mother realized it would be a bit anticlimactic since the bike had arrived early. She decided a birthday party would put some interest into the big tenth.

She enlisted me as co-organizer, and we started work on our guest list. We ran into only one snag: Yvonne Wright.

The problem I had with Yvonne was that she had decided I would be her boyfriend, and I simply was not ready to have a girlfriend or be a boyfriend. Her openness relative to the subject was causing me some discomfort; Harold and Boo were delivering some ribbing on the subject and I saw it as only getting worse. To invite Yvonne would surely encourage her and motivate my pals to increase their kidding about my having a girlfriend. But Yvonne's interest in me simply added to my mother's appreciation of her good taste in boys, and consequently, Yvonne *would* be invited.

Looking back, what could Yvonne have seen in me? The simple answer had to be that I was the oldest boy in the Pacific Lane neighborhood, which I'm certain had to be the sole qualifier.

Yvonne was a vivacious girl, a powderkeg of personality, uninhibited and precocious—way ahead of me. My interest in sports and my neighborhood chums left no time for any kind of actual relationship with a real girl. Sheena was enough for now. I would have to think of something to smooth this situation out.

Among the invited guests would be Glen Mitchell, who lived only a long block from Pacific Lane; that put him on the rim of the loop. He was a sports fan from birth. Beyond our evolving improvised games we played in the street, he followed the world of football and baseball with a notebook full of statistics, which was always being updated. There was no major league baseball in California; our baseball was represented by the Pacific Coast League: locally the L.A. Angels and the Hollywood Stars. Glen knew the names of all the players and their averages. He was my age, blond, with wavy hair. I wondered why Yvonne couldn't have picked him instead of me.

The latest inordinate and significant sporting fact Glen had recorded in his diary was that the 1942 Rose Bowl game, traditionally played in Pasadena on New Year's Day, had been moved from the blacked-out Pacific Coast to Durham, North Carolina, home of the Duke Blue Devils. The Japanese might have sunk our fleet, but they couldn't stop the Rose Bowl game. Heavily favored Duke had lost to Oregon State. Glen was happy about the upset and looked forward to baseball season. The games would be played by presidential consent, but almost all the good players would be in the military services. Baseball became almost comical, still he concentrated on the stats. I wished he would concentrate on Yvonne, but he had even less appetite for romance than I did.

So with my mother's guidance, the invitations were processed and personalized, ready for hand delivery, about a dozen in all, mostly for the neighborhood with a couple outsiders. There were lots more kids in the neighborhood, but these represented the present core group.

Grandma Ellen baked me an angelfood cake, my current favorite; the kids began to arrive. Plates of cookies, penny candies, and popcorn were distributed throughout the house and were pounced upon as soon as the small, ornately wrapped gifts had been delivered. The gifts would be inexpensive; it was understood and accepted. Had expensive gifts been required, birthday parties would not have been popular. Harold's gift was tubular, an easy guess: a comic book. He would already have read it, of course.

Soon all the invited guests were present, with one notable exception: Yvonne Wright.

Other girls were in attendance: Gloria, Martha, Daisy, and Patsy Tucker. It seemed dangerous to have Harold and Gloria in the same room at the same time, but we took the chance. It was almost a disaster! Gloria's hair was arranged in tube-like curls, and as she prepared to take a bite of cake, Harold pulled one of the irresistible tubes. The cake hit Gloria's chin instead of her mouth, and Harold ran for cover behind my mother. Harmless enough, but we could literally see the fire in Gloria's eyes as she fought to control her uncontrollable temper. Martha began to babble platitudes in an attempt to prevent the explosion. It was a brave act on her part; everyone knew there was a live bomb among us, and unless Harold was delivered to the sacrificial altar, God only knew what would happen.

My mother realized the only remedy was to force Harold to eat humble pie. She brought him before Gloria and told him to apologize. We were all accustomed to obeying adult authority, and Harold was no exception, so he dutifully told Gloria he was sorry—but the expression on his face and the look in his eyes was easily read by everyone in the room, especially Gloria. The situation was not over, only postponed; Gloria would kill Harold at the first opportunity, and Harold was convinced it had been worth it; whatever price he would pay, Gloria would have to catch him first.

The emergency behind her, my mother inventoried the room once more. Yvonne Wright still was not present. Since there had been no note of regret, my mother was still expecting an appearance.

We did a "Pin the Tail on the Donkey" game, a guessing game, and I opened my packages. Comic books were popular, and Harold was engrossed during the opening process. Everyone seemed to have a good time.

But after everyone had departed, my mother remarked about Yvonne's absence. I acted preoccupied and headed for Harold's and Boo's houses to see if they had changed into their play clothes. I had the party behind me and Yvonne hadn't caused me grief. Good party!

✖

Wash day!

As my mother replenished my clean underwear supply, she noticed the corner of an envelope. It had a familiar look about it, and when she turned it over, the name "Yvonne Wright" was revealed. She was aghast. Her heart ached for Yvonne, who obviously was terribly hurt to be the only excluded kid. Her heart ached even more to think that I could be so cruel to one of the neighborhood kids.

In a rare display of defensiveness, I accused my mother of insensitivity relative to my discomfort, attempting to label Yvonne as an aggressive, pushy person making my life miserable. Why couldn't she leave me alone?

My mother would have none of it, informing me that Yvonne's attention was, in fact, a real compliment, one that I didn't deserve, and that I had not only been cruel, but I had exhibited an immaturity that she thought I had grown beyond. She was really upset with me, and I wasn't used to that.

I asked what she expected me to do, tell Yvonne that I didn't want a girlfriend?

"That," she told me, "would be a good start," adding that I might think about a sincere apology for my inexcusable behavior and bad manners.

I checked in at Knappy's, chancing that Yvonne would not be there. I needed a safe haven, but it would not prove to be so, for Martha and an older girl who went by the nickname "Red Death" were there and could tell something was wrong. Both girls were light years ahead of me in the race to maturity.

So I told them the whole story. Martha just stared at me like I was an idiot, but I knew I was in real trouble when Red put her head in her hands. My spirits took a major nosedive. Yvonne would hate me, Martha would hate me, Red would hate me, my mother didn't like me very much, and as the news spread, who *would* like me? I began to imagine that even Lucky might consider me to be a despised rat as well.

Red looked up at me and asked me how I felt about all this. I responded that it didn't take a genius to realize that I had screwed up royally, but Red continued to look in my eyes and asked again, "But how do *you* feel about it?"

I got the point. "I feel like I hurt Yvonne a lot," I said.

"You're going to have to tell her that, LeRoy, and right away." Red was not going to let me off easy. She looked me in the eye again and held her gaze; I was defenseless. With a sigh, I got up and headed for Yvonne's house.

She didn't want me for a boyfriend anymore.

✄

So my previously unblemished neighborhood social life had suffered a direct hit by a bomb I had dropped on myself. Word had gotten around about the invitation and the apology, so things were returning to normal. But a cloud loomed on the school horizon, and it hit with tornado force. I don't believe anyone warned us kids this was coming; I don't think the adults thought to. We were oblivious of any threat to our classmates. We went to school and expected everything to be okay, war or no war.

We talked about the war a lot, and most of the boys were crazy about airplanes. Fifth grade aviation art exploded into our notebooks where lessons should have been. Pages were filled with our aerial dogfights; always an American plane would be disposing of a Japanese or German plane. Flames licked at the Axis pilots, their ships pointing groundward in a final dive to doom.

I drew such a picture, a flaming enemy plane with Japanese insignia, and had a wonderful thought: Chizuko and Sakio could write Japanese characters, which would give more realism to my drawing. I had no idea that it would be unpleasant for the girls. I wasn't insensitive; I was ignorant of any problem. I really made no connection between the girls and our conflict in the Pacific. As far as I knew, none of the kids was treating them like the enemy. They were our friends—just two kids.

I sensed a negative reaction from Chizuko, who supplied the secret foreign cipher, the last words the enemy pilot would utter, and she politely requested I not ask again. It was clear that I had committed a faux pas, and I began to piece it together in my mind. Under no circumstances could I view the girls as the enemy, but they *were*

Japanese. What was going to happen here? I began to feel bad and worry.

What happened was terrible and tragic. We kids didn't know, and of course we were not consulted. As usual it was after the fact when we found out, but sometime during the month of March in 1942, Chizuko and Sakio's desks were no longer occupied. They had never been absent before, so something had to be dreadfully wrong. What was wrong was this: on February 19 President Roosevelt had signed an executive order which removed our classmates from school and from their homes to a "relocation camp" somewhere. I never saw them again.

We were advised that Japanese people represented a threat to the security of the nation, but how could Chizuko and Sakio be spies or saboteurs? They, of course, were not.

"*All* persons of Japanese descent" were relocated. They had simply been uprooted from their businesses, homes, and farms and incarcerated. No trial, no appeal. A baby was as guilty as a male adult. No distinction.

I was really sad, but ten-year-old kids move on quickly, and because feelings ran so high, perhaps these Japanese Americans were safer out of the general population. It was an excuse I never heard, though; the reason always centered around spying. Chizuko and Sakio, "master spies." I couldn't grasp the concept.

The adult population did not seem to share our sadness in the least. In their defense, the war was more real and less romantic to them, and they could not distinguish between Japanese and American Japanese. They were all just Japs!

What happened to Chizuko and Sakio? I fear I'll never know, but there were times I could have used their volunteer tutoring. Emotionally, I've never really recovered from their disappearance. I still miss them and wonder how we could have treated them that way.

✖

Our appetite for heroes was being nourished daily. A bomber pilot named Colin Kelly flew his crippled plane into the funnel of a Japanese ship to become one of the first stories of heroic personal sacrifice. It was only the beginning.

Pictures of General Douglas McArthur graced magazine covers and picture puzzles. His image superimposed over a backdrop of an American flag was everywhere. Our blood was infused with large quantities of patriotism; we oozed it.

The "E-for-excellence" flags were flying proudly below Old Glory at "defense plants," a general designation given any company involved in war production. More incentive than award. American workers were girding themselves to do the very best they could. No one wanted his mistake to be the reason for a soldier or sailor to lose his life. People were really motivated. "Do your part" was a popular call to arms, and the answer was coming through loud and clear.

Women were going to work with a new sense of self-respect. They were wonderful factory workers and their contribution was an essential factor in the unprecedented production effort that ultimately made all the difference in the direction of the war. Ships, planes, tanks, guns, and ammunition rolled off production lines in an unending stream, and as the war effort devoured raw materials, things got scarce on the civilian front. The war effort needed to be fed first.

An example that would have serious consequences for all us kids was sugar. No food item was more important than sugar. Howdy's began to present a different fountain menu as a large percentage of food and beverage production went directly to "feed the boys."

Cokes and Hershey Bars were under-the-counter items—scarce, that is—and meted out very selectively. Soon meat, shoes, and gas were rationed. There was no civilian automobile production. Only military vehicles were being produced, so if one had a 1942 auto, it would be the newest car in the neighborhood for years.

But morale was sky high and grumbles about scarcities were rare. Almost any complaint or unreasonable request elicited the phrase "Don't you know there's a war on?" and the argument was over. Enthusiasm and determination far outstripped the depression one would expect to accompany war.

A blue star in the window meant someone in the household served in the armed forces. Many windows were decorated with the symbols. A gold star was a most sobering sight. Someone had died. A household had sacrificed a loved one "to preserve liberty." Gold stars were not rare as the war ground on, but America remained focused.

We learned a lot of geography as a result of the war. Places we had never heard of became raging battlegrounds where many brave soldiers died. No one ever figured out why someone died and someone else didn't. It was a mysterious selection process with no apparent reason to it. Parents, wives, and survivors would never figure it out or stop trying.

A lot of women took a step beyond the defense plants and joined the armed services themselves. They were in every branch, and we boys did some rethinking of our attitudes about females. Given a chance, they would have volunteered for combat. We had to admit it. They were impressive, on a path far beyond what was expected. And volunteers, every one. But combat? Let's not get crazy.

As things got tougher for Americans, one thing was very clear even to us kids. We were, as usual, better off than anyone else. Our kid counterparts in England, Russia, and even Germany were living lives of terror, although we convinced ourselves that we would prefer to be more involved, too. Easy to say from a great distance.

The movies were the icing on the cake. War movies were being turned out with the same production speed as everything else, and actors were almost given hero status because of the roles they played. In the case of John Wayne, that is exactly what happened.

The movies were, of course, propaganda, thinly disguised and willingly ingested by a victory-hungry nation. We kids believed every frame of film and eagerly awaited the next installment. We sat in the darkened theaters enthralled. No one was noisy or rowdy; we were too involved.

There were air-raid drills, blackouts, air-raid wardens, searchlights, and anti-aircraft installations to remind us of what war *could* be.

One trick the government missed was using ten-year-old boys as aircraft spotters. We were better at it than anybody. We could identify anything that flew—and we had young eyes. Distance was no problem.

If an airplane picture appeared in the paper or a magazine, it was cut and pasted in a scrapbook in a heartbeat. We were always alert for the sound of aircraft engines overhead.

It was a Saturday afternoon when I heard such a sound and

looked upward to see a P-38 Lightning disappear briefly into a cloud and then reappear with one of its engines on fire. The pilot turned the stricken plane westward out to sea, and a moment later a parachute blossomed, a tiny figure hanging from its shroud lines.

I was momentarily stunned and immobile. Then adrenaline shot through me and I ran for my beloved bike. When that pilot landed, I wanted to be there. To see a real in-the-flesh P-38 pilot was too good to be true. A P-38 was more beautiful than Hedy Lamar, Lana Turner, and Betty Grable combined.

There was no time to locate Harold or Boo or anyone. I could lose sight of the 'chute and miss the event completely if I hesitated, and I knew one thing: I was the only kid in the Pacific Lane area who had seen the flaming plane. This would provide bragging rights for a long time in the neighborhood.

The pilot was descending quite a distance to the southwest and I tried to maintain a straight line to the probable point of impact, but I couldn't do it. I had to zigzag through streets and alleys, nearly crashing into trash cans and jumping curbs as the pilot dropped lower on the horizon.

Suddenly I noticed that the pilot was drifting toward me, and before I knew it, he passed high overhead, the breezes guiding him in the exact direction from which I had begun this chase. I reversed my direction. Madly pedaling, I retraced my trail and soon lost sight of my pilot as he dropped below the roof lines.

As I arrived at my starting point, I could see in the field some 200 yards away a group of kids and a pilot with an armload of spent parachute. He was getting into a jeep. In the blink of an eye, the jeep was going, leaving the crowd to disperse, excitedly discussing the adventure of the year.

I had blown it! I had been the only neighborhood kid to miss out, and now I would have to hear all about it from Harold, Boo, Richard, and everybody else. No thanks! I parked my bike and went into the house to pout. Moments later Harold and Boo were outside my door calling for me to come out. What the hell; I'd have to hear about it sooner or later. Let's get it over with.

To my surprise, I came through the re-hash process pretty well. As far as I could tell, I was the only one who saw the pilot "hit the

silk"; in fact neither Harold nor Boo had seen the plane, a major part
of the adventure. By the time my piece and their pieces were viewed
together, things were about even. We all sang the Air Force song together: "Off we go into the wild blue yonder, climbing high into the
sun," three junior P-38 pilots.

What a day, what a song, what a war. I sang with all the gusto I
could muster—"We live in fame or go down in flame...."

✖

My singing voice had me in some trouble at school—trouble
once again from a direction least expected, or so it seemed to me.
How can you prepare?

One of the teachers had a flair for show business and decided to
do an "Andy Hardy" and "put on a show." A schoolwide "Star Search"
was underway for her operetta, "The Early Bird Catches the Worm."

I had never made a secret of my voice; I just never thought of it
as dangerous. I went around singing all the time. I had, however,
never considered doing it from a stage with a spotlight focused, along
with an auditorium full of student and parental eyes, directly on me.
I definitely was not ready for that, but I was discovered without any
audition. Too many people had heard me sing.

As the program moved along, I was swept along with it, looking
for my exit opportunity, which continued to elude me. This was not
an optional activity, I learned. "Compulsory operetta," a new concept
in the educational system. As if I wasn't having enough trouble with
my math since Chizuko and Sakio were gone, now I had to deal with
stage fright, which didn't seem like a fair fifth-grade emotional anxiety ordeal to me.

My parents were no help at all. In fact, the prospect of my talents being showcased really brought out the stage mother in my
mom. She was madly enthusiastic and the pressure points now
doubled. This was not good. Maybe Harold would have some ideas
to get me out of this. I sure hoped so. I had "jello stomach" again.

✖

Speaking of singing, the music of the day was laced with war-in-
spired songs. On the comedy side was Spike Jones with "In Der

Fuerer's Face," but most were concerned with painful separation: "I'll Walk Alone," "Ain't Misbehavin'," "Don't Sit Under the Apple Tree with Anyone Else but Me" and "There'll be Blue Birds Over the White Cliffs of Dover."

There were lots of purely patriotic songs too—some, like "Over There," resurrected from WWI, I think. "Praise the Lord and Pass the Ammunition," "Comin' in on a Wing and a Prayer" and "Rosie the Riveter" were examples of the new musical wave of the flag. Kate Smith would make our blood run red, white, and blue every week with her theme "God Bless America." The killer was a Christmas song entitled "I'll Be Home for Christmas"—one of the saddest songs ever written—and Bing Crosby tore our hearts right out of our chests when he sang it, whether we had loved ones in the armed forces or not. There was no problem identifying and empathizing; everybody was in this together.

"Victory gardens" began to spring up everywhere. Some were the effort of an individual family and some were shared projects. We had one in the lot between our house and Shultz's. My dad had a bit of the farmer in him and it showed. Our crops were really impressive; beans, peas, potatoes, carrots, beets, radishes, onions, and squash thrived. I loved to see the process work. Pretty miraculous, I thought. It represented a bonanza for my grandmother and her fabulous cooking.

I received a pet rabbit for Easter—a doe—and soon my dad had us in the rabbit business. Before long he added chickens. I saw an opportunity. Since I really liked our expanding mini-farm next door, I decided to ask my dad if I could replace my magazine sales with garden and livestock responsibilities. I carefully rehearsed and presented my proposition.

He would consider it, but I got a serious lecture on the nature of my responsibilities to the project. "These are living things," he pointed out, "plants and animals. Neglected, they will die by the hand of the person charged with the responsibility to sustain them, and once dead, they are irretrievable—lost forever." This was sobering stuff and food for thought. We were talking daily, not weekly, chores, and if I failed, it would be disastrous.

The up side was the difference between a job I liked and a job I didn't like, and I had an ace in the hole: my grandmother. She had more farmer in her than any of us, and I knew she would retain some involvement. She was in her glory when she was in the garden. One thing was certain however; I would never be able to subrogate any portion of my responsibilities to her. She was immune in the presence of any guilt of any kind.

So there it was. The option of "neither of the above" was not open to me. If I wanted out, I faced escalating work *and* responsibility; but if I stayed with the status quo, it was a lifetime of *Ladies' Home Journal* sales.

✖

Mrs. Carter (no relation to our earlier murder suspect) was convinced I was one of her important operetta participants—not the star; the sixth graders were to get first crack at the major roles—but she insisted I sing for her, and she liked what she heard. What I wanted was a crack to crawl out through, but there was a vocal solo shaping up in my future. What in the hell was I going to do? Going around singing, even singing on request, was no problem, but in front of a real audience, an auditorium full of people? I would faint dead away with the first note. My heart was pounding just thinking about it.

So home I went with sheet music for "The Early Bird Catches the Worm." The setting was a barnyard and all the participants were farm animals. The plot involved a rooster that had a bad habit of oversleeping, failing to wake the farmer and the other animals in the morning. As a consequence, the barnyard schedule was never in synch.

The farmer, as well as the animals, was unhappy with the rooster, of course, and my song was sung by one of the disgruntled young chickens politicking for the key job. It all seemed to me like the kind of thing that could stigmatize a young lad for life. "Chicken LeRoy." Who could live with that? Harold would think of something, I thought, but before I could get anything out of my mouth, Harold said, "Guess what? I'm going to be in an operetta!" A big help he was. He couldn't carry a three-note tune, and he was thrilled to death about being on a stage. I should have guessed. When a real crisis came along, I never had an ally, or so it seemed to me.

I went over to Knappy's for some thinking space. I *had* to escape this thing; I couldn't go through with it. Gloria was there and thought my dilemma was hilarious. Gloria was growing up much faster than I was. I wished she would go barechested à la Jovine, but I knew there was too much to bare.

But there it was again; what I saw as a disaster was a source of comic relief to others, and I seemed once again adrift on a troubled sea in a leaky life raft. Was I to go through life like a fly in an inkblot, entertaining everyone around me with my struggles, to finally lie exhausted and helpless—my final moments more fascinating than tragic?

When the miracle arrived, I got a little more religious. My ideas and escape attempts had played out when, during an early rehearsal, my voice cracked. It just kind of took off in a tonal direction as if it had a mind of its own. I started again as directed, but it was no use. I couldn't depend on my voice at all. My brain was sending musical impulses that my vocal cords could not obey. My voice had begun a long process of change—just in the nick of time. God had intervened; he had at last decided I suffered too much for a fifth grader.

So Mrs. Carter replaced me with another kid chicken and demoted me to one of the extras—a generic chicken, faceless in the flock. Harold and I would have similar roles in the operetta. The important thing was, no solo. I had dodged a very large bullet. My mother, however, was noticeably upset to be deprived of this great stage mom role opportunity.

❊

My cousin Gene, the oldest of the few cousins on my mother's side of the family, had come to live with us. His father had been killed in a railroad accident, and he had recently graduated from high school in Nebraska. He was very smart but not very healthy. I loved having him live in our house. He was a heroic figure to me merely by the fact that he was nineteen years old. That fact, however, constituted a real problem: the draft.

Gene got a job at National Supply Company right away. He could have worked just about anywhere, except for his draft status.

He could ace any employment test.

It should be understood that while our patriotism ran sky high, having a close, loved relative of ripe draft status was emotionally difficult to deal with. Additionally, we just didn't think Gene was physically able to undergo the rigors of basic training, not to mention combat. The Army wasn't too sure either, but they liked Gene's mind too much to just give up and 4F him.

Gene was called for a number of physical examinations and special tests. He was always sent home and told to stand by for notification. We were all apprehensive and serious as we waited for some word after each episode. Notification would always come in the form of another physical.

Finally Gene was instructed to report for duty and assigned to the Army Air Corps, a situation that would ordinarily have resulted in a state of ecstasy for me, but we were all too worried about him for me to fantasize an image of Gene at the controls of a B-17 or P-38. He was sent, however, to a cadet training school in Colorado.

After only a few months, Gene's frail health became too apparent and he was discharged "for medical reasons." We all breathed a great sigh of relief, but to my great disappointment, we didn't get him back. He remained in Colorado to attend college.

Ultimately Gene became Gene Hakanson, Ph.D.—a doctor of psychology and director of the Department of Psychology for the State of Kentucky, but not before he returned to us for three years, which provided me with some well-directed scholastic confidence-building input. He helped teach me that I wasn't so dumb. He played the older brother role better than a real one, and when he married and moved away, I missed him a lot.

⌘

Robert was a kid alone in a lonely world. As I've indicated, I sometimes felt that way, but Robert's case was the real thing. To me, the world was full of kids, but for him, there was no one. He was invisible, nonexistent, except to a few cruel kids who thought he was funny.

Robert suffered from cerebral palsy, and the kids did not know how to deal with him and it, so they generally just completely ignored him. No taunts, no cruel remarks; he just didn't exist for most of us. We busied ourselves when he was around.

Once, in the cafeteria, he lost the entire contents of his luncheon tray as I watched. I was so mortified for him, but my reaction was predictable—I left the scene hoping that someone would come to his aid and hoping that his tray was replenished, but my contribution was *zero!* I didn't even want to think about it.

I felt sorry for him, but I was just not endowed with the wisdom required to change anything. Most kids did feel sorry for him, but did nothing. His exaggerated and uncontrolled movements were at once pathetic and sometimes comical in a morbid way. The terrible part of it was that we just knew that he was a really nice kid, but what to do about it? He couldn't participate in sports. He couldn't even run, let alone catch or throw with any hope of getting close to a target, be it person or barn! So how to make a connection?

What did we have in common with Robert? The obvious answer was that we were all just kids, including Robert; but we weren't smart enough to see that. Robert just seemed too different.

I was stunned to learn that Gloria had done something positive about Robert's isolation. It seemed so out of character, since she was in great measure a loner, quiet, moody and withdrawn, not a favorite of the teachers. She had approached Mrs. Carter and argued for a place in the operetta for Robert—if he agreed, that is. Gloria correctly saw an opportunity for Robert to be a kid among kids, if just for a short time.

I was so impressed and I told Gloria so. She was serious and grown up about it and suggested that if Robert hesitated or declined, I should try to influence him. I was a player in a noble cause for the first time and I really felt good about it. I wished I had thought of it first.

Robert didn't hesitate. He was thrilled to be included. Rather than just let my involvement lapse, I told Robert how glad I was that we would be in the operetta together—thus breaking the unintended wall of silence. An unforgettable feeling of warmth flowed over me as Robert's unmistakable enthusiasm radiated through me. This was one of life's real moments, watching Robert become included for the first time. Were these his first really happy moments?

※

I had passed from the rank of magazine salesman to the nobility accorded to fledgling farmer and rancher. No more *Saturday Evening Post* and, more importantly, no *Ladies' Home Journal* to peddle. I was a happy farmer.

My dad was spending considerable time building rabbit hutches and chicken coops. The multiplying rabbits were increasing my chores proportionately. Surely there was a limit to the number of rabbits I would be expected to take care of. But they kept coming. Never mind; it was not hard work and I loved animals—even the chickens.

We no longer bought eggs. The hens were laying as fast as we used them. Considering my grandmother's baking prowess, that was saying something. The little red meat we were able to obtain was augmented with chicken and rabbit, which we had in generous supply. The killing, however, was left to my dad. I couldn't handle that.

Soon word got around that we had a surplus of rabbits, and people began to knock on the door. Word further circulated that our animals were especially healthy. It was a simple case of proper care. I kept the hutches very clean, and the feeding and watering routine was done on schedule. Our reputation increased our sales. Because the rabbits were producing a profit, my dad began to pay me a percentage, and soon my percentage was considerably more than I could have achieved selling magazines.

I was surprised to learn that these animals, essentially just elements of the human food chain, had subtle personality differences. In the case of roosters, not even subtle. It was an example revealing that upon closer examination there is almost always more to be seen and learned.

There were lots of victory gardens, but not any others in our neighborhood. The vacant lot between the Shultzes and us was the only appropriate spot, and it was ours to use.

I had chosen correctly. I was in business and making money. Best of all, this time I really loved my job. None of my friends had much responsibility, but I liked my deal, and I don't recall being envious of their idle time.

Operetta night arrived, as we all knew it would, and since my
role was so generic, I had no particular apprehension—that is, not
until we received our costumes. I couldn't believe we were really expected to wear these things. We were the dumbest-looking chickens
one could imagine. Essentially they were made of tan jersey underwear, legless and armless, with yellow crepe paper feathers glued to
them. We had yellow paper chicken feet taped around our ankles,
and we were topped off, literally, with red stocking caps tied in a
fashion designed to look like combs. We looked hilarious, not by intent.

Only the knowledge that I was one of many barnyard chickens
gave me the courage to emerge from my dressing area, and when I
did, I ran right into Yvonne Thomas. She was really cute and I had
found myself thinking about her every once in a while lately. She
looked at me and smothered her laughter, releasing only a chuckle,
but that was more than I needed right now. I was beet red.

The girls somehow looked infinitely better than the boys—
Yvonne especially—and when she said to me "nice legs," I knew this
was the image of me she would have forevermore. Forget about
Yvonne, I thought.

The scene backstage was chaotic. Harold was putting on a pre-
operetta show, acting like a chicken with its head cut off. I was attempting to be invisible; he was trying to be the center of attention.
Most people were nervous, and some of the boys were humiliated
like I was.

Robert wore his costume as proudly as if it were a Marine dress
uniform, and oddly, he seemed more controlled and more coordi-
nated. His involvement, his inclusion, had somehow empowered him
to reach within himself to, in great measure, suppress his handicap
temporarily; he was in another zone.

My parents, disappointed that I wouldn't be singing solo, nonetheless came to see me on stage. I preferred not to be seen by anyone.

There was a large keg, stage center. It was a stage on a stage for
the barnyard oration, and when, prior to curtain time, Mrs. Carter

called "places," I headed straight for the barrel—not the audience side, I assure you—and there I would remain throughout the entire performance.

My parents searched in vain for me, wondering where I could be. Parents recognize their own kid, even in a chicken suit. Their chicken-kid was not to be seen.

While I hid behind the barrel, Harold stole the show. He strutted around the stage chicken style, elbows back and thrusting his head forward with each step. He scratched the stage floor with his paper clawed foot and then cocked his head to "one-eye" the scratch.

People were laughing when they weren't supposed to and I could see Mrs. Carter offstage looking none too happy. The lead rooster was being seriously upstaged; the audience didn't care if he overslept or not.

Yvonne was a hen, and as she wandered around the barnyard, she spied me obviously hiding out and flashed me a knowing smile, but I didn't know what it really meant. I guess it meant she knew what an insecure "wimp" I was; she was just too kind to say it.

God, was this the longest school play in history, or what? Minutes seemed like days; would this thing never end? Harold hoped not, and Robert, too, was having the time of his life wandering around like Yvonne, preparing for the big scene with the foxes. At that moment, I pictured Robert's parents in the audience and figured they must be even more ecstatic than Robert was. It helped pass the time to think about them, and it took my mind off my own parents.

The rooster that couldn't wake up in the morning was an insomniac by night. His crowing in the middle of the night alerted the farmer during an attack by a nocturnal pack of foxes, and all the sleeping chickens were saved; a fool turned hero. Why didn't that ever happen to me? The hero part, I mean.

Once or twice I peeked from behind the barrel and my father spotted me. For many years he kidded me. I was the "egg behind the keg." I was surprised he took it so well; I expected him to be mad. I decided to take his kidding well, too, and I began to notice that it was more fun to laugh about things than to agonize over them. My dad and I were having fun with it. Mom, who took everything better than either of us, just put the whole thing behind her. The egg behind the keg had not provided any maternal bragging rights this time around, but there would be another day and she would be ready. Music lessons loomed in my future.

✖

My mother's best friend and chief rival relative to bragging rights was Edith Pierce. Her son, Myron, like me, was an only child. The big difference was that my mother urged me; Myron's mother commanded him. The pressure on Myron was constant. His instrument was the accordion. He had a tin ear and no natural rhythm, but his determination and willingness knew no bounds. He was a real "gamer."

By comparison, I was oozing musical talent. My situation was much more democratic, but my mother made no bones about the fact that I *would* do *something* with my aptitude. It was pretty much a matter of elimination. It was decided that I would be exposed to everything until I settled the issue by indicating some long-term interest. Once again, "none of the above" would not be an option.

Dancing was the worst! Once again, fate stepped in disguised as a sprained ankle. I didn't sprain it dancing, I sprained it at play; but dancing was out. It was the sprained ankle from heaven. God had intervened again, but made me pay the price in pain. It was worth it!

Before I got into a mess like that again, I decided to make a move to a compromise position. I requested clarinet lessons; I liked Benny Goodman. A lucky guess, I guess, because I kind of liked the idea of being good at something musical, and the music teacher liked the tone I was able to produce early on. Tone was everything in wind instruments. If you had it, they wanted you.

Given a bit of talent, the secret to success is perseverance, and the secret to perseverance is a little bit of success. For once I felt as if I had landed on my feet in one of these compulsory situations. I was really doing okay, which fueled my enthusiasm.

I would have been more comfortable if my progress hadn't resulted in yet more pressure on Myron. Edith was relentless. Myron toiled; I just pretty much blew air in and reasonably pleasant sounds resulted. I was getting the feeling Edith didn't like me anymore.

Myron labored quite oblivious to my competitive presence. He pumped and pulled, pressed keys and pushed buttons frantically, and produced common songs in unrecognizable form. God, it made my teeth hurt. Mostly though, I felt sorry for Myron and resentment toward Edith. I was beginning not to like her either.

As we advanced in ability, we began to migrate toward a "recital." I had no problem with it, unlike the barnyard solo singing. I had practiced and felt quite prepared. By recital time it would be automatic; my concern was for Myron.

We often practiced together, and a recital was not where I wanted to see Myron anytime soon. His accordion was beginning to assume a life of its own in my eyes. The damned thing was alive and like an extraterrestrial creature. It had control of Myron. The notes spilling out and over seemed more like signals to some distant planet than music for earthlings to dance to.

Myron's mother, too, began to appear to me like an interplanetary mastermind, manipulating the consumption of Myron's earthly identity, fusing Myron and the accordion into a single horrible squawking, wheezing mass. I had definitely been reading too much Buck Rogers and Flash Gordon, but I couldn't help it. I just couldn't figure out where this was going. Was Myron's life to be ruined because he couldn't play the damned accordion? What could I do? I was just a fledgling clarinet player.

I loved the song Myron was preparing to recite—"Lady of Spain," the classic accordion piece. My "Clarinet Polka" was coming along okay, so I began to spend a little time on "Lady of Spain." What a song. In private I sang it, too. It was a better song than "Clarinet Polka"; easier to play, too. "Clarinet Polka" required both accuracy and pace. Polkas just don't sound right when played like a waltz.

✠

I was getting a real education with my farming, and it made me feel wonderful to be among thriving animals and plants. It isn't that it underscores the artificiality of manufactured goods and material things, it just emphasizes what is real. Seeing a bean plant break through the earth while seeming too fragile to accomplish such a feat—its stem should have been broken in the process, but it wasn't. How fascinating and puzzling and mysterious. It was really inspiring.

Hens do not lay multiples of eggs in a day. I had assumed they did and I know that many people continue through life thinking so. To lay one egg a day during her season is feat enough; it is not an easy chore, as I learned from peeking as the process took place. When, on rare occasions, a hen lays two eggs in one day, it is noteworthy indeed, the kind of accomplishment my grandmother enjoyed—the extra effort deserved special praise, she felt, and so it did.

The experience of gathering eggs is somehow unexplainably rewarding. To lift the lid of the nest box and find this perfect object—to hold this still warm little miracle right in one's hand—made a special impression, even at my tender age. Most significant was the feeling that I was a contributor to the phenomenon. How marvelous. I loved it all. There was a farmer trying to come out of me, too.

Pygmy chickens are called "banties." The word when written is "bantam," but they are always called "banties." They tend to do everything better than their normal-size counterparts, from setting on fertile eggs to parenting following the hatching. The great bonus they provide is how tame they become—pets with a purpose—the little hens, anyway.

My two banties, Mr. and Mrs. Murphy, were like a barnyard illustration of the conventional gender roles—she the tireless mother, he the "cock-o'-the-walk," the barnyard boss, strutting arrogantly all day long.

I would never have a job I loved more or one that gave me as much satisfaction. I understand why people must farm in spite of the hard life, the disappointments, the disasters. The rewards are mystical, and felt so thoroughly, internally and externally. Few pursuits in life can match the feeling, of that I am certain.

It puzzled me that my pals were not as fascinated with it as I was, but it was no problem for me to leave the group when duty called. My reception was always enthusiastic. The animals knew where their dinner came from, making me a popular guy at feeding time.

ⵣ

My "Clarinet Polka" was becoming flawless. Perhaps the tempo was not quite "Goodman," but I had it down pat and it sounded pretty darn good.

Myron's "Lady of Spain" was still mostly energy rather than music. He was hitting the right notes in robotic fashion, but his timing was nowhere to be found. One could usually guess what he was playing but only when the occasional familiar passage kicked in, and the much-needed minor miracle occurred and just as quickly evaporated once again.

While Myron practiced, I fingered my clarinet silently and was noticed by the music teacher. She asked me if I knew the piece, and when I nodded, she said, "Play along."

At first Myron looked surprised and he missed a beat or two, but soon he took off again and wonder of wonders, he began to sound better. Instead of random note playing, he began to match my tempo, and the composer's intent surfaced for the first time. The Lady of Spain revealed herself from the recesses of Myron's gaudy device.

At the end, even Edith stood speechless. She was not alone. Myron was waiting for a reaction from somewhere, but like Lincoln's Gettysburg Address, the audience was reduced to stunned silence. Myron and I didn't expect applause, but the silence was confusing. Time was at a standstill it seemed. And then Edith was clucking and fluttering around Myron, full of praise and encouragement, for the first time ever in my experience. She was joined by the music teacher, and as I glanced at my mother, I received a look that said more than words could express. I had, I realized, just done a musical good deed that affected everyone in the vicinity. For the first time, Myron's colossal efforts were resulting in praise from a source that had only produced criticism in the past. And for the moment, at least, he was too stunned to enjoy it. Everyone else was enjoying it immensely. Myron was not comedic in his musical ineptitude; he was pitiful. Everyone had felt sorry for him, and watching the scene taking place on the rehearsal stage sent a warm feeling through us all as Myron began to actually glow in our eyes. This was a good day. Edith's reaction seemed a bigger miracle than the duet. We watched and savored what we thought and hoped was Myron's latent musical talent switch go to the "on" position. In our hearts we knew better.

School was going okay, and I was grateful that Yvonne Thomas did not seem to dwell on the "chicken" incident. In fact, she seemed more friendly than before, a curious situation. I had expected her to share my humiliation with the entire female class population, but she didn't. Perhaps the answer was with Sheena and Bill. Sheena's friend Bill was a bumbling klutz and Sheena never seemed to tire of his oafishness, so maybe Yvonne just had a Sheena complex. That was worth some quiet moments of thought. It occurred to me that Yvonne would look pretty good in a leopard-skin outfit.

Actually, airplanes were more important than girls. While some kids just drew generic planes, mine were identifiable. My P-40s had air scoops under the propeller spinners and the sharks' teeth of the Flying Tigers, my P-38s had twin booms, and my P-51 Mustangs had clipped wingtips. The enemy planes had the characteristics of Japanese Zeros and Messerschmit 109s. The Germans said "Himmel" when they were mortally hit, and the Japanese said "banzai," no matter what the occasion. I had recovered from the loss of Chizuko and Sakio, but when I was engaged in these artistic, vicarious dogfights, their faces would float back into my consciousness. I didn't talk about it, but I was pretty sure other kids missed them, too. I was equally certain there was little sympathy at the parental level, so the matter just kind of fell away in silence and reentered my thoughts at unexpected times.

Everyone was overwhelmed with patriotism, which fueled the magnificent united effort to win the war. The downside was that the cause was justification for many unjust actions on both sides, as is true with any war. This war would produce atrocities of mind-bending proportion, all justifiable in the minds of the perpetrators. "Patriotism," "national interest," "the cause," "just following orders"— excuses that would attempt to justify awful things.

Just on the outskirts of town we had a major surprise occur. Before the townsfolk had time to react, a prisoner of war camp was established for Italian soldiers. At first there was real apprehension, but soon we learned these were the happiest people in America. For them the war was over, and to a man, they were glad.

We had heard that the Italians were reluctant to be fighting the Allies, but we saw it firsthand from these cheerful guys, who would

wave and smile if you made eye contact while driving by the minimum security camp. They were digging meaningless holes and filling
them up again, obviously glad to be doing it. Before long, they were
even brought by truck into town and allowed to shop for necessities.
There was never an incident, and I have often wondered if they went
home after the war. I'm sure they had families to return to, but boy,
were they happy to be in America, where no one was shooting at
them anymore.

The Italians may not have been as reluctant to participate as we
felt, but they were not even remotely as impassioned as the Germans
and Japanese, there was no doubt of that. They were ferocious fighters—fanatical, in fact.

∎

About mid-semester something happened that made me forget
Yvonne Thomas—almost made me forget about drawing airplanes.
Marie Atkins arrived at our school in my class!

Marie was from Oklahoma, as were lots of folks in Southern California in the 1940s. Boy, I thought, she was gorgeous. It was love at
first sight. The trouble with falling in love for the first time is that
you don't know what to do about it. Or is it that way every time? In
any case, I was lost, clueless. I never felt so alone. Whom could I talk
to about this?

A second problem with a cute girl new to the class: *all* the boys
fall in love with her.

Intuition is a useful thing. I intuitively felt it was too risky to talk
to an adult about this. Ridicule and humiliation lurked behind every
adolescent developmental landmark. Surely one's first love was a
prime target, and I had missed a checkpoint or two in the past. Caution. Proceed with caution, my subconscious warned.

Who else? Not Harold. He lagged behind, younger, and my ex-
ploratory probing relative to Jovine or Sheena never went anywhere.
Not likely he would be any help with this new development. Where
would his experience come from? Forget Harold.

So here I was again, in the middle of the ocean, in my one-man
life raft. Which way do I paddle? While I was trying to decide, the
ache was getting more pronounced and competition arrived in the

form of the most popular boy in our class, Richard Bayless. Talk about complicated. Two new emotions almost simultaneously: love and jealousy. Is this fair? I'm just a kid.

I couldn't talk to my folks, Harold was no help, and the person I most wanted to tell was totally unapproachable. I wanted Marie to know, but I'd kill myself if she found out. I was on an emotional roller coaster, scared of the ride I was on, but not wanting off. The feeling was getting familiar, but it never seemed to get any more comfortable.

⌑

Recital time arrived, and I had missed a couple of rehearsals because of chicken pox. No problem; more opportunity to practice. The itching took my mind off the heartache of my secret love, too, though my imagination sometimes ran amok.

Marie and Richard Bayless assumed the personae of Dorothy Lamour and Jon Hall in the movie "Typhoon." I was relegated to a cameo role, a poor, crippled, and pitiful silent admirer of the Island Beauty. But at the moment I was focused, ready to ace "Clarinet Polka," and then leave it behind forever. Ten million times is enough to play any one song in any one lifetime.

The distressing news was that Myron had reverted to his pre-duet level of competence, and once again my anxiety level rose on his behalf. I had not been asked to repeat the duet performance that had been so effective. God, I would die a thousand deaths during his ordeal. Under no circumstances would I make eye contact with Edith during his performance.

The first performer was a piano student, a teenager who did a nice job, who played two pieces and got lots of applause.

I was next. I played the polka about as well as I could, and the audience graciously applauded enthusiastically. At Mrs. Evans' request, I followed with "Beautiful Dreamer," my dad's favorite song, and played it without a mistake, probably for the first time ever. It wasn't particularly difficult, but because my dad was always listening with a critical ear, I never played it very well. I really did okay and wished that Marie could have seen and heard me. In my mind I had contrived hundreds of ways to impress her, knowing they were merely pipe dreams. I probably would have dropped my clarinet if she had actually been in the audience and I had known it.

Another accordion player followed me and belted out "Granada" and a polka. He struggled but finished strong and, once again, the audience was gracious and forgiving, applauding with gusto.

Myron was due on stage, but something was wrong. He was skipped over, and another piano student filled his slot on the program. Where was Myron?

Where was Myron was right! He had disappeared and Edith was about to have a heart attack! I joined the search. Down in the band room, in a corner to the dark side of the upright piano, I found him, hugging his knees, terrified. He was in his accordion uniform, satin balloon-sleeved shirt, and to my astonishment, he had on lipstick and rouge on his cheeks. He was crying, of course.

"What's wrong?" I asked. But of course I knew. It was just the best I could think of.

No response, so I said, "Myron, you have to come out and get it over with. Your mom will be here in a minute." No response from the catatonic Myron.

I heard footsteps behind me and I knew it would be Edith. I was right.

Both Edith and Myron were very blond. They were presently very red of face. Myron had been crying, and Edith was furious and crimson. When Edith commanded Myron to come out, there was no possible way for Myron to resist—no escape, the lioness and her cub (more like her prey) in tow.

I ran ahead to tell Mrs. Evans, the music teacher, what was going on—and I had an idea. I suggested, of course, that I play the piece with Myron. Mrs. Evans accepted my idea with enthusiasm, but then I watched her expression change and I knew what she was thinking. Would Edith concede—a duet instead of a solo? The crisis was expanding as time was running out.

Myron looked as if he were being led to the chopping block. Edith's will was limitless in its scope, but the target of her energy was unable to respond. Myron would never be able to do it; it was a physical and psychological impossibility.

There was not much time left. The last performer was on stage and Mrs. Evans was appealing to Edith, who looked as if she were surrendering rather than compromising. She acquiesced, surprisingly, after only a brief pause, while I worked on Myron. Myron may have been reduced to jello, but he was no fool. He knew instantly it was the best deal he could expect, and he jumped at my offer. The deal was struck. "Duet City!"

Edith was to exert her dominance one more time, however—not on Myron, but on me. She took me aside and told me to play as softly as possible. This was, after all, Myron's solo piece. I nodded agreement. Actually, I only had one volume level. If I blew too hard, I could expect a squeak; too soft and the note sounded like it had hair on it. I would just play.

So out on stage we went. I let Myron play the introduction since it was little more than a flourish or two and joined in as he took off on his quest to get it over with.

Lightning struck again, just as it had before. Myron was watching and listening to me, placing his notes on top of mine with enough synchronization to sound like a duet, and it sounded like "Lady of Spain!"

When we finished together, the audience went nuts. They thought two kids playing together was a much greater feat than a solo. They wanted an encore. Wow! This was an even better idea than I thought.

"Lady of Spain" was the only song Myron knew, so we played it again. More applause, but also more control. They liked it, but not enough to risk hearing the same song a third time. That was okay with me too.

I could tell Edith was confused by it all—the audience appreciation versus the lost solo opportunity. Congratulations and compliments pushed her over the edge, and she took on the posture of proud mother—the moment Myron had been waiting for. He had dodged a bullet and was basking in the glow of his mother's apparent satisfaction, a rare commodity in his young life. He hardly knew how to react.

I was getting my strokes too. After all, I had been out there as well. My mother looked at me like I was the Boy Jesus. Life was good!

Marie hadn't been at the recital, so my musical hero status did not extend far enough to really do me any good where I needed it. Marie had become the nucleus of my universe.

Harold and I were drifting apart a bit at a time. We were in different grades, I was more athletic than he, and there were no chores, music lessons, or practice time in Harold's daily schedule. Besides, he had no apparent interest in girls. In short, he remained the luckiest kid in the world.

We did have the neighborhood and comic books in common, however, and these were not minor connections. Divorcing myself from Harold would certainly put a negative slant on my status at Howdy's, too. I didn't want that! Finally, and importantly, Harold and I were *friends*. We had fun together and rarely, if ever, really disagreed or argued. We never fought! So as we drifted our different directions, we would be bound together. Our bindings would stretch but never really break. Real pals are pals for life, aren't they?

That friendship, however, was not occupying much of my conscious thought. I wanted to find a way to nurture a friendship with Marie Atkins. I needed a way to draw positive attention to myself—a way to make Marie think I was really neat.

Leaping out of the bushes with my clarinet and launching into "Beautiful Dreamer" was not, I knew intuitively, a reasonable scheme to upstage Richard Bayless. Good, but not good enough. I knew that fantasizing was safer than the jeopardy represented by actual approach, but like a moth to flame, I felt myself losing control. All I could think of was becoming Marie's boyfriend. But how?

I needed an opportunity to be a hero. Then Marie would cling to me like a leech. But how does an eleven-year-old boy become a bona fide hero?

My imagination was working overtime. If I were a fighter pilot, I would tell her how dangerous my patrols were and relate the strong likelihood that I might not return. "Let's make every moment count," I would say. Then the breeze would rustle the curtains and waves would crash on the shore. Later she would cry as I climbed into the cockpit of my P-47 Thunderbolt and disappeared into the perilous night sky, perhaps never to be seen again.

Richard Bayless must not enter my thoughts. The mission would require every ounce of concentration I could muster. Flyers who worried or let outside influences penetrate their determined purpose were not likely to come back. But I was at 15,000 feet, short on fuel, and out of ammo, while Richard was there working side by side with Marie at the flight center. How do you compete with that? Life can be so unfair!

Perhaps if I played John Alden to Richard's Miles Standish.... But no, that was far too dangerous. Marie would probably welcome the confirmation of Richard's interest and where would I be then? Life was getting complicated again. Why couldn't Marie just fall in love with me?

✥

In Torrance in the 1940s, grammar school ended at the sixth grade and high school began with the seventh grade. There were no junior high or middle schools.

To a sixth- or seventh-grader, high school students were adults, and of course, the seniors seemed old enough to be our parents.

I had been recruited into the high school band while still a sixth-grader, so I was getting a firsthand preview of the difference between these two academic worlds. Geographically, they were only a block apart, but what went on within the two was like Earth and Mars. I had some real questions about the readiness of my classmates and me to fit into this place. For one thing, I noticed that every hour everyone moved to a different area. Would we be able to figure out where we belonged?

There were some huge people in the band; members spanned all the grades and came in all sizes and shapes. I was unquestionably the smallest and youngest. The french horn player was the largest and loudest and rowdiest.

I sat next to the flute player, also a very large person, but as it turned out, gentle as a lamb and warmly friendly. He had a great calming manner and he was an immense aid to my adjustment to this foreign environment. He even taught me a little about playing the flute.

Prior to the arrival of the bandmaster, the scene was pure chaos. Some people would be tuning their instruments, but mostly the big male members were just being rowdy.

When Mr. Sauter entered, nothing changed much, but when he stepped to the podium and tapped his baton on his music stand, a transformation of miraculous proportions took place. Everyone sat down and stopped whatever racket they were making. Everyone's attention was directed respectfully at Mr. Sauter. Adding to the phenomenon was the fact that Mr. Sauter was a soft-spoken, mild person who could not possibly have forced these people to do anything they did not want to do. I was awed by his control over this riotous group.

As time went by, I understood. These people *wanted* to be in the band. It was fun. If they were uncooperative, they were out—period! A band required infinite coordination to sound even reasonably decent, so one either behaved or he lost his seat, and getting back in was nigh impossible. To be kicked out of the band would be a disaster—to have instrumental skill and no forum in which to display it. No wonder the rowdies behaved. I stress the masculine gender because the girls were simply no problem—always under control and well behaved. Why was that, I wondered?

I acted more like the girls. I was intimidated by these large, elderly people and by the fact that I was a smallish, youngish person. But when the baton set the tempo, I was equal to many and better than some; I just wasn't confident enough to be rowdy.

I was under Mr. Sauter's wing. Either he was protecting me because of my age or he thought I had some promise. Probably a bit of each. He had to be a little bit impressed. After all, I was just a grammar school kid good enough to play in the high school band.

Our music was comprised of school songs to be played at assemblies and sports events—classic marches and "Pomp and Circumstance," which we would play at commencement ceremonies.

Playing the clarinet took on new meaning. Until now, I thought playing solos was what it was all about, but being a part of a band was downright thrilling. I had never felt the satisfaction of contributing to the "big picture" before. It was a great feeling and I really loved it. Playing marches makes one's heart beat faster.

The best was yet to come: football season.

The band did not have uniforms, but they did have these wonderful looking maroon-on-the-outside, silver-on-the-inside capes, to be worn on game day. Capes were the trademark of our super-heroes, so they seemed unique and made me feel special. There were small military style caps to match. We would march onto the field and into our fifty-yard-line bleacher seats playing the encouraging school fight songs. Would she be there? If she was there, would she notice me among all these gigantic people? Did she like football? Did they play football in Oklahoma? Perhaps it would be better if she didn't notice me, I decided. I would surely look like a midget mascot recruited for comic relief. The more I thought about it, the less confident I was about the "impress-Marie-with-the-band" program. My hero status would have to emerge from some other source. I just appeared too insignificant. In fact, among all these large, mature people, I hardly appeared at all. I wasn't much bigger than my damned clarinet.

✸

Richard Bayless was a whiz at making model airplanes, both flying models and solid models. He would bring them to school to display his skills to the class whenever he finished one. I noticed Marie was impressed; everyone was impressed. No one else brought anything of an impressive nature, so Richard was a clear winner—no competition and lots of exposure.

I tried to build the damned things, but it took loads of patience and precise work done in stages. I was short-goal oriented in the main. If I was going to build a model, it needed to begin and end the same day to keep my attention. At the end of the day, what I had to show for my effort was a far cry from Richard's productions. To expect them to actually fly was preposterous! Besides, how do you keep glue from getting all over everything?

The solid models were a total mystery to me. The kit contained a block of balsa wood that could have been the basis for a Grumman Wildcat or a cow for all I could tell. Forget solid models! I could draw airplanes better than Richard or just about anyone else in the class. However, when I left my efforts in conspicuous places, it was obvious Marie didn't possess the critical eye necessary to judge my drawings as compared to others. To Marie, all the boys drew airplanes. So what? Instead, one day a picture of Gene Autry's horse, Champion, drawn by Marie Atkins, was taped to the blackboard. It was terrific! It looked like the grandest, proudest horse I ever saw. There was, taped beside the drawing, an eight-by-ten glossy of Gene Autry with the inscription, "To Marie in grateful appreciation for the picture of Champion." It was signed, "Gene Autry, 'King of Cowboys.'"

Marie explained to the class that Gene Autry was her favorite movie star, and that she had drawn a picture similar to the one on display here and sent it to her idol. His response was the eight-by-ten, obviously cherished by Marie. This, I thought, was good information in case I ever got up the nerve to have a conversation with Marie—especially since I was a serious Roy Rogers fan and thought Gene Autry sounded like a sick cow when he sang. That opinion would be pushed out of my mind. What if I had said that to her? What if I said *anything* to her is more like it. Maybe if I went around singing cowboy songs? Would she notice?

I went around humming "Deep Within My Heart Lies a Melody." I didn't know many cowboy songs.

I didn't think about Marie's nipples. To me, Marie was not ordinary. She was infinitely pure; she probably didn't even have nipples or other common, vulgar body parts either.

Marie ate lunch like the rest of us, but I was sure that was all. Surely she was exempt from other humiliating body functions the rest of us mere mortals were forced to endure. Could Marie even consort with ordinary people who indulged in common, humbling processes? Surely the gods were grooming this perfect creature for something special. Neither Richard nor I was worthy. How dare he? I began to see myself not as Marie's boyfriend, but more as her subject, wishing only to dedicate myself to her bidding. My loyal servitude, I thought, might qualify me to sample her favors—like holding her hand, for instance.

✖

I forgot to feed and water the animals!

My dad had waited until the last logical moment—before their day ended—and fed them. He was very upset and disappointed. So was I! He was not talking to me—the worst kind of punishment. The longer it went on, the worse I felt, and I was in the pits.

There was no sympathy, not even any advice from my mother. She knew this was out of her jurisdiction. My dad had exiled me, and she knew better than to soften the environment. Parental team-work—they were consistent and I was accustomed to it. I would have to suffer and plead before this would be over, and it served me right!

My mind, of course, had been somewhere else and time had slipped away. I had ridden my bike over to Marie's house on the out-skirts of town on the chance that she would see me and come out— the classic "I just happened to be in the neighborhood" ploy.

Marie did see me and she did come out. She waved. I waved and peddled away purposefully as if on an errand, my heart pounding—a lost opportunity. It was after dark when I got home and I was still fantasizing about what I should have done and said, but my head cleared for an instant and I knew I was in big trouble. The animals were not nocturnal.

Would the animals survive a day without food and fresh water? Probably, but productive animals laying eggs and bearing offspring are busy. Their metabolisms race, and they cannot be neglected. Their dependency is total. I had failed them and my dad. This was a bad day.

I would, of course, apologize at every opportunity, and I would, of course, be ignored. I would, of course, display even more consci-entiousness, but that, of course, would be expected.

Time, contrition, and attitude—the ingredients of forgiveness. It was all I could expect.

The silent treatment was not lasting. My dad knew I was honestly sorry. But sorry was not enough. Forgiveness given too easily deemphasizes the incident, minimizes the importance, and my dad was resolved to let me know how serious this affair was. Hadn't we talked about this very possibility? My responsibilities were not a child's busywork, they were the major league. I had asked for man's work, I had been forewarned, I had persisted, and had been awarded the job. I had impressed him and convinced him, and now I had failed him.

That is how he explained it after my third apology. Things began to get better, but forgiveness would come in degrees. I realized that I had better make some changes in a hurry.

This love business was going to have to come under some control. I could not allow my head to be so muddled that this happened again. I couldn't conceive of the consequences of that! Either Marie Atkins was going to be my girlfriend or I was going to give up the whole idea. How important were girls anyway? Maybe I was getting ahead of myself with this girl stuff.

EX

Anna had made me one of her world-class chocolate malts. Harold had told her about my troubles at home, and she was sympathetic. She was permissive by nature, and her attempt at presenting a tough exterior was seen through by everyone who really knew her.

Harold had no chores; Anna felt it was kind of cruel to make kids do work. That attitude left Harold a free spirit—no responsibilities and lots of time on his hands. He wasn't doing very well in school; there was just no discipline to provide direction, and it was not in his nature to generate his own discipline.

Surprisingly, I didn't envy Harold in this respect. I needed the kind of parents I had. Oh, there were moments when I felt somewhat smothered, but for the most part, I knew my more structured lifestyle was an advantage. This was not a display of any great preadolescent insight. After all, Harold essentially was fatherless. I wouldn't want that, and I knew it was not Harold's choice either. But I welcomed their sympathy for my present situation even though I was undeserving, completely unworthy of any consideration in respect to the pickle which I alone had arranged for myself. They didn't ask how I came to forget my chores, and I certainly did not volunteer that information.

The final part of my malt was stuck to the bottom of the heavy glass container. I tipped it way up and suddenly it lost its adhesion and splattered all over my face. How come everyone was watching whenever that happened?

EX

Gas rationing had effectively eliminated an American pastime—the Sunday drive. It was nothing more than riding around, going nowhere in particular, for no specific reason, just a Sunday drive. It provided the basis for a phrase that was popular for many years after Sunday drives disappeared as part of the American way of life. If someone was driving slowly and totally unmindful of the cars behind him, he or she was considered a "Sunday driver," regardless of the day of the week.

Even if one's allotment of gasoline was enough to permit a Sunday drive, to drive for pleasure was almost considered unpatriotic, and no one wanted that label. Sunday driving became as scarce as sugar. The tradeoff was to go visit someone. That made the drive more necessary—or less unpatriotic, whichever one preferred.

So it was that one Sunday we had enough gas to plan such an outing—a visit to some friends in Glendale.

We had traded our dependable little Ford coupe for a 1938 Chevrolet sedan. It would prove to be a match for the Ford in every way—a terrific car. It was certainly a more comfortable car, especially when my grandmother accompanied us, which she almost always did. We never would have fit into the Ford.

Traffic was no problem. Gasoline was just too scarce to produce heavy traffic.

As we made our way to Glendale on the nearly deserted road, we began to overtake a car moving slowly and alternately moving from the right-hand lane to the left-hand lane.

My dad watched warily for a while and then decided to pass the car, but as we drew side by side, the car veered into our lane and brushed our rear fender. My dad had increased his speed and had almost averted the accident, but not quite.

The car slowed and fell behind as my dad reduced his speed. I expected the driver of the offending car to be in the most trouble I could imagine. Knowing my dad meant knowing that this guy was about to feel knuckles tattooing his nose and chin. This was not going to be pretty!

I watched through the rear window as the driver emerged from his car. He could barely walk, staggering toward my dad with a big smile on his face as if he were about to meet his long-lost best friend.

There was another man remaining in the car. He appeared to be sound asleep, completely unaware of anything going on.

My dad looked at our car to assess the damage, then took a firm hold on the man and returned him to his car. He opened the car door and firmly deposited the man behind the wheel. The man continued to smile crazily the entire time, as if he were having a really great time. He was oblivious to the peril, had my dad acted in the manner I expected. He was oblivious period!

As my dad walked back to our car, I got the impression the driver was going to join his passenger in slumber. We drove away; he didn't.

I was really stunned. In my opinion, the guy had somehow dodged a really big bullet in the form of my father—a man with a low flash point and very quick and efficient fists.

My dad read my thoughts and his remarks were directed mostly to me. "The man," he said, "was very very drunk—unaware of where he was or what had taken place." I had no problem with his description of the man's condition, but so what? He went on to instruct me that I should always avoid any hostilities with people who were crazy or drunk.

The damage was minimal, but that was not the point, I was advised. A crazy or a drunk might pull a gun and shoot someone before he even knew what he had done, and surely before the surprised victim could react. The other possibility was that because of their condition, you might do far too much damage to them—not good either. I was really impressed and that advice has remained prominent in my mind all my life, even though I never really needed it.

I had always thought my dad's temper was in control of him, so I saw a different side of him and I thought it was great. I admired his physical strength, and now I admired his control and wisdom.

I looked at my mother and saw an expression of relief and approval. She was always laboring to elevate our respectability quotient, and a fist fight in the middle of the road was not on her top ten list; but she knew it had been a distinct possibility—perhaps a probability.

At this moment, and until some event caused a reversal, my saintly mother elevated my dad to a state of familial grace. All was well in the Swigart world as the dependable Chevy, a slight crease in the rear fender, bore us efficiently to our friends' home in Glendale.

The events of the day fell away as I learned the Streamliner train passed right behind our friends' rear fence. During the course of the visit, two or three went by, and I thought it was thrilling. Trains can really make one's blood heat up and heart beat faster. To think Superman could stop a speeding train—what a feat!

✹

There weren't any Japanese people left in town. Like Chizuko and Sakio, they had just vanished.

The Ranch Market, owned and operated by Japanese people, was closed and soon converted to a furniture store. What really happened to them, we kids would not know for years. Our attention was distracted. Besides, President Roosevelt said it was "for the sake of national security." President Roosevelt was above everybody but God, so the matter was settled.

We were certainly not without minority people, however. We had a large population of Mexicans and they had lots of kids. They were considered second-class citizens. Discrimination was overt, and many of the Mexican kids were angry and aggressive as a result of their treatment. They were considered intellectually inferior, which caused additional resentment. Often they spoke little English, sometimes none at all. Our teachers spoke no Spanish, so these kids, in defiance of logic, were considered slow learners and relegated to "the bungalows," where their self-esteem sank lower and lower. It was unlikely any of them were actually "slow"; at least I never met a slow one and I came to know lots of them.

The Mexican children were, in fact, very interesting kids. While learning a new language, they enjoyed teaching theirs to anyone who showed any interest. Funny I don't recall any of us whites going out of our way to teach them. They were doing all the work for both sides.

Anyway, when I brought the Tapia brothers, Edmund and Robert—Edmundo and Roberto actually—home one day, they were instantly converted to either "Castillian" or "high Spanish" by my mexophobic mother. I don't mean to be hard on her. These ideas were the nature of the townsfolk. It was both "areal" and "eral."

Mexicans were, well, "not like us." Castillians and high Spanish came much closer.

Well, these two ragtag delightful "Castillians" were great fun to know, and rather than just waiting for me while I did my livestock chores, they pitched right in and helped, and they knew what they were doing. They had done a lot of farm work in their young lives, and our common involvement cemented our relationship. Perhaps for the first time they felt "connected" to a white kid.

So by the time my dad got home that evening, instead of the yard having one well-organized hour of work performed, it had three. It was spotless in every respect, and he was really impressed. His feigned anger was falling away more rapidly than he had intended.

I accepted my dad's complimentary remarks and waited until dinner to confess that I was not the sole source of the pristine appearance of the yard. My dad was, if anything, more impressed than ever, a surprise to me because my dad was not a very tolerant person at all, but he worked with a number of Mexicans, and the steel mill was an equalizer. They were good workers.

In addition to gaining my dad's approval, I had learned to count to twenty in Spanish and that *poy-yo* (the Tapias had no clue how to spell it) meant chicken.

Counter to the fear that the Mexicans might attempt to assume a white role, the truer case was that I had taken a step toward honorary Mexicanism. Had my mother realized that, I'm not sure she would have handled it, but I really didn't recognize it either, so there was no problem. The Tapias were around a lot, and Harold, Albert, and the other neighborhood kids were glad for the new element they represented.

It was very curious to me that our food was peculiar and not especially appetizing to them. When they shared a sample of their food with me, I understood why. It was so different and so good.

Our differences were contributing to our interest in one another rather than pushing us apart, and we were having lots of fun comparing our lifestyles. They thought peanut-butter-and-jelly sandwiches made of white Wonder Bread were too odd and unappetizing to even consider as food. I noticed that it probably was not a very good idea to think about it too much at that.

I was not an adventurous eater, but the aroma emanating from the Tapia kitchen overwhelmed my reticence and I found their food to be spicy and greasy—in a word, delicious! They tended to wrap food in pancakes they called *tor-T-yas*. It did a job Wonder Bread could never attempt. You could wrap real sloppy stuff in it, fold the ends, and you had a leakproof tube full of food. It tasted great!

Mrs. Tapia was big enough to make three of my mother. Her skirt went to the floor and could have served as a tent for us three boys. She spoke little English, but she had no difficulty making me feel welcome. That she was really nice was instantly apparent.

Consistent with her appearance, Mrs. Tapia felt we should always be eating. Robert and Edmund just ignored her urgings most of the time, but she stayed after me. I was too small and skinny, I suppose, which inspired her nourishing instincts. Unlike her boys, I was not comfortable refusing or ignoring her offerings, so I would nibble courteously and try to move out of range as quickly as I could. Even so, a visit to the Tapia casa usually resulted in an untouched meal at home that evening, a condition not appreciated by my grandmother, who nearly always cooked something especially for me. I felt bad when her efforts were wasted.

The Tapias did not live in "Pueblo," the Mexican settlement at the northwest edge of town. They lived west of town, not far from the Cheesicks' little farm. That they did not live in Pueblo was a great relief to my mother, who would have struggled with the "high Spanish-Castillian" classification had they lived among the "common Mexicans" in what was, of course, a ghetto.

The Tapias' house was small, but most of my friends lived in small houses, so that aspect did not distinguish the family from any other. What made them different was that entering their house was like walking into another country. They were Mexican people in a Mexican environment, and I was fascinated and comfortable there.

For reasons I could never really quite understand, I was much more at home in their house than they were in mine. They were welcome there, they just didn't or couldn't relax.

Our cultural differences, which often fueled our curiosity and fused our friendship, had the opposite effect sometimes. American football and European soccer created a chasm we couldn't seem to narrow enough to cross. The Latinos had no interest at all in our sport, and our attempts to participate in theirs were reduced to shin-kicking contests, "Whites against the Mexicans." It wasn't pretty!

My bike gave me great mobility, so I got to know the Tapias very well and began to pick up more and more Spanish in the process. Although they called her "Mama," she was their "*madre*," and I became one of her *niños*. Robert told me it meant "boy," but she intended it to mean "baby."

Upon my arrival, Mrs. Tapia would summon me and surround me with her bulk. She loved to hug kids. At first I was a bit embarrassed, but it seemed so natural that my inhibitions fell away and I just surrendered to what was hardly an unpleasant welcoming.

Then it happened—one day with everyone present in the kitchen, including the two older Tapia girls, Mama hugged me so hard I farted quite audibly. I was mortified, but only for a few moments, because when their laughter subsided, it became apparent that they thought it was the cutest thing I had ever done. My adopted status was somehow elevated by the incident—a mystery to me since overt passage of gas was not considered acceptable among the ladies in our house. If it happened, it happened quite by accident and was ignored by all, as if no one had heard. It was the fashion in which all embarrassing or uncomfortable situations were addressed by my family. To this day, I can't relieve a gas pain in the presence of another, be it friend or wife, nor can I really look a handicapped person in the eye.

But the Tapias handled it like a celebration of the end of my "visitor" status and the beginning of a "belonging." I was *família*. Nevertheless, on future visits, I made certain that while enroute, I purged myself of any potential for a repeat performance. I was satisfied with my present status in La Familia Tapia. My vocabulary now included the word *pedo*.

✗

My decision to deemphasize my infatuation for Marie was easier said than done—like most things in life, it seemed to me. I was determined, however, that I would not be again so preoccupied that I would do stupid things and get into jams like the last one.

But when Marie came into view, I would drift in and out of control, not realizing I had been adrift until my head cleared and I stared at a blank page of notebook paper where there should have been something ready to submit before the final bell of the day.

Frantically I would attempt to do an hour's work in fifteen minutes, and the result, as one would predict, was less than perfect. Barely presentable was more precise. Before long, predictably, my teacher was on my case and then, out of concern, in touch with my parents. Oh great! Just as my life was smoothing out, "pothole city."

Since I couldn't give a logical reason why I was so preoccupied in school, my mother became suspicious that my participation in the band was a bit over my head—too much to handle at my age and "perhaps we should wait until you are in high school, a bit older and more capable of handling the program."

I begged, I cried, I pleaded, I assured, I won! My mother relented with my promise that she would hear of instant improvement, schoolwork-wise. A reprieve, but potholes abounded.

Not for long, really. The next day the class was buzzing with the news that Richard Bayless had *kissed* Marie. *Kissed* Marie? What the hell was going on? I had fantasized *talking* to Marie. In wilder moments my imagination conjured a vision of us *holding hands*. Richard Bayless had *kissed* her? No, no way. Kissing a girl in the sixth grade was comparable to raising a family in adult life. Surely it was a wild rumor with no basis in fact.

✄

Once again I was tumbling, as if caught in a "pounder," into the uncharted waters of an unknown and turbulent sea, about to be drilled head first into the sandy bottom.

Every day I spent in the sixth grade moved me closer to high school. At least I wouldn't be facing this newest ordeal alone, or would we all be facing it alone?

My exposure and participation in the band was both comforting and disconcerting. I felt it would help to know people when the time came, but at the same time, these people seemed so mature and independent, so confident and capable. I didn't feel that way at all.

Rumors flew, and none of us had enough hard information to

know if we should believe them or not. One that was particularly up-setting was that on rainy days the gym classes moved indoors and became co-ed dances. According to those in the know, the dance terminated with the boy kissing the girl's foot. Talk about your basic stomach ache!

We all looked forward to having lockers. Somehow having one's own locker was exciting all out of proportion to the reality of it. I guess it was just that grammar school didn't have them and high school did, so they took on a strange symbolism.

The downside was the rumored penalties for forgetting your combination or your locker location: swats! You would get a swat with a paddle if you left your locker open, two swats if you forgot the combination and someone had to search the files for you. The swats were administered by members of the Varsity Club, big guys who took pleasure in their opportunity to inflict pain on their victims.

I have had a recurring dream all my life in which the central theme is a forgotten combination or a locker location that seems to move with a will of its own—it is never where I recall it should be. Huge people with gigantic paddles lurk in the shadows while I struggle to locate or open my locker. I wake up in a sweat. The dream never ends; it just reverts back to the beginning for another replay at the earliest opportunity. I wish I could get my swat and have it over with, but in the dream it looms as ominous as a beheading.

Anyway, if what they said was true, the damned school was a swat factory.

Chew gum—a swat.

Late for class—a swat.

Fail to strip for gym—a swat.

Fail to shower—a swat.

Poison your teacher—a swat!

I finally caught on. Things got wildly exaggerated whenever nobody knew anything and got worried. Additionally, lots of people liked to see other people squirm, especially if they did some squirming back in their initial exposure. My advantage, once more, was the band. The flute player seated beside me, Ralph Prime, was a gentle giant, always kidding and happy. After imposing some minor "squirm" on me, he told me what I thought I knew, that if I played by the rules, high school posed no real peril, and I would do just fine.

I had plenty of time to think things through these days since my infatuation with Marie had hit a major pothole. In fact, there was no more infatuation. Richard and Marie could just as well be married.

The big rumor had turned out to be no rumor at all. Not only had Richard kissed Marie, but just for good measure, at lunchtime she had kissed him back. Everyone had seen this one, including me. Girls were such drips, and they made a wreck out of a guy. I had even tried to like Gene Autry. No more girls in this fella's life, I thought. But before the thought had completely dissolved, I found myself wondering if Yvonne still thought of me as "Charlie Chicken," the egg behind the keg.

✠

I wasn't the only one with glass-detector feet. Boo's little brother, Richard, had stepped on a shard from a Coke bottle and had really done a number on the sole of his leatherlike foot. He had a tin can rescued from the garbage, and was collecting the gore as it oozed from the wound. It was his thought that he would contribute the rapidly coagulating mess to the Red Cross, thus aiding the war effort. We all knew how important blood was to the thousands of brave, wounded servicemen, and I was reluctant to inform him that such contaminated blood would surely hasten, not postpone or prevent, a tragic and early death. But I hated to see him waste his time and the flow of blood, which he encouraged rather than discouraged. I was a bit worried that he really might bleed too much.

Patsy Tucker wandered on to the scene, and when she saw what Richard was doing, she wrinkled her nose and stuck out her tongue to indicate her disgust. She was not as reluctant as I to set Richard straight, but he had already invested too much time and effort to pay heed to Patsy's exhortations on the subject of common sense.

Patsy was a real firecracker—full of energy and always in a good mood. She had lots of freckles, was slightly on the plump side, and everybody liked her. How could you not? She was completely uninhibited, and sometimes I was lost for a response to her unexpected, off-the-wall commentary. Today was one of those days.

Patsy informed me that she was thrilled because Yvonne Wright, who was developing in the Sheena sense at a rapid rate, had assured Patsy that she could expect to have ample and pointed breasts like hers. Now how was I supposed to respond to that? Why did people do that? Was she looking for a second opinion? Was I supposed to suggest she remove her blouse and allow me to examine her budding little, potentially large, pointed boobs? I thought not. Instead I told her I intended to start lifting weights and I thought my arms would one day be as large and muscular as my dad's. It seemed like a comparable condition to me. Would she be satisfied? She appeared to be puzzled for a moment and cocked her head to one side and apparently decided she had chosen the wrong audience, or the wrong subject, or a brain-dead individual to discuss this with.

Typically Patsy, she didn't just let it go. She asked me if it made me nervous to talk about boobs. I asked her to tell me about her experience in Hawaii, in a desperate attempt to redirect the conversation.

Patsy had actually been living in Honolulu in December of 1941 and could relate some firsthand information about the "sneak attack." It made her a celebrity among us "war fans."

Patsy saw through my clever verbal manipulation instantly and started to giggle while I started to blush. She said the air raid scared her so much it made her nipples shrivel. I responded that I needed to feed my animals and dashed away while she laughed at my awkward response to her titillating remarks.

Let her talk about that stuff to Richard, I thought. They were both a bit loony today. I hoped Richard was not going to bleed to death, though.

Lots of the neighborhood girls were maturing. Daisy already had a Sheena-class chest, and Gloria and Martha were wearing brassieres, I could tell.

I was worried enough about Richard to detour back to Knappy's to let Albert know what was going on. I gave the customary "Booooo" call and waited. It usually took two. A second call, but no response. On the third try, Albert's mom came out just as Harold arrived. She announced that Boo didn't live there anymore! We stared. What did she mean?

After a long moment, she reiterated that Boo didn't live there anymore. "Boo is Albert!" If we wanted Albert, "Call for Albert."

So that was the last day we called him Boo. Knappy had spoken, and Boo was nonexistent. He had metamorphosed into an Albert. So, Albert, let's go see to your little brother before he bleeds to death. I just hoped Patsy wasn't still there.

✸

Pacific Lane had a clean look and a fresh aroma. It had just stopped raining, and as the sun's rays burst through the gray overcast, Harold's voice broke the post-rainstorm stillness.

I was being summoned in the usual manner, and as I emerged from my back door, Harold was pointing to a spectacular rainbow. We both gazed in wonder, literally. We had no clue how the phenomenon was produced other than it was a rather common miracle. God's magic on display.

Harold announced, matter-of-factly, that a rainbow was God's promise not to destroy the world by flood. It sounded reasonable to me, not to mention comforting. I really liked the concept.

Just how Harold might know what God intended about anything was a mystery. He sure didn't learn it from church or Sunday school. Spending any part of a weekend confined, for even an hour, would never appeal to Harold. That didn't mean he wasn't a strong believer, though. The fact that the Axis nations were so godless made us more faithful. God was the ally we had who would, regardless of day-to-day setbacks and disappointments like Pearl Harbor, Wake Island, Bataan, and Manila, ultimately punish the evil enemy. It was axiomatic; God was on our side. We repeated the phrase often.

So I welcomed Harold's religious "axiom" since it validated what we needed to be true: to fight so hard, as our brave boys had done and were doing, only to drown along with all the bad guys, seemed unlikely because it was unfair, and if God was anything, he surely was fair. Harold had it right again, regardless of how he knew.

The adult population wished they had our faith and confidence. The knowledge that the enemy was dying in greater numbers than our brave boys was not the victorious testimony they sought, but resolve overcame occasional moments of nervous doubt, and they strove to participate and contribute, with all their vigor. America's awesome production capability was up and running, the world changing with breathtaking speed. Industrial evolution was visible to the naked eye.

Also visible was the ice truck which had just entered the neighborhood. The ice man, a big, strong guy with tools that reminded us more of weapons, was in fact a pussycat. Invariably there would be, within easy reach, a few ideally shaped ice shards for us kids to dash out and grab from the bed of his truck as he toted a large block of ice into the nearest kitchen. He would knock and enter, all in one motion. Never would he wait to be admitted, and never was the back door locked during the day. A block of ice was not something that could be left on the doorstep. His key to enter was a sign in the window or on the screen door which had a three-letter message: "ICE." He was an endangered species, facing certain extinction with each passing day.

One by one the ice man's customers were replacing his service and product with "Frigidaires," an icebox that didn't need a block of ice. It was never clear to us why his ice was so pleasant to suck on, but before long, he and his uniquely recognizable truck would cease to visit, and the daggers of ice would disappear with him. Hot summer days would not be the same. We were unable to conceive of this simple evolutionary equation and never even considered that the ice man, the Good Humor man, the Helms Bakery man, and the Fuller Brush man would vanish from our neighborhood, from our lives. They were as real and solid as brick and mortar to us.

The almost mind-bending music that accompanied the Good Humor man, all in sharps and flats, had a charm, and more importantly, it had found a place in our lives. Given a vote, no kid would opt to banish him; but one day he was gone. "Merrily We Roll Along" would never sound so sour and leave such a sweet memory. Unlike the dinosaurs, no bones were left behind to remind future generations that these critters once existed, roamed among us, and enriched our lives with their presence.

✺

My Uncle Hack was one of those "nicest guys in the world" that every family seems to have one of. If the world were made up of Hacks, there wouldn't have been any wars. There might not have even been any arguments!

Uncle Hack appeared at our back door one day with a cardboard box in his arms and tears in his eyes. The tears weren't streaming down his face, but a couple had escaped his burning eye sockets. My uncle was in great distress and my anxiety level soared. He was a wonderful uncle.

This was a new experience for me. I had never seen an adult male cry before and I had no clue what disastrous event could cause such a reaction. Nothing, I was convinced, could have brought my father to tears; it was impossible to imagine such a thing.

The box contained a dead cat, and its remains represented the essence of the disaster. Hack was crushed. It was the scroungy little family pet, Scamp. Personally, I always thought it should have been named Tramp. Its coat looked as if it had been previously worn by a cat of a different size and shape that had failed to take proper care of it. But Hack and his wife, Doris, liked Lucky and I loved Hack and Doris, so I always acted like I cared more for the cat than I actually did. It was not a difficult role to play since I really liked all animals, even Scamp.

It was a different story with Lucky and my dad. Lucky acted like Scamp didn't exist. Like my dad, she didn't really care for cats anyway, but this one didn't even rate a glance. My dad was a "dog man" all the way, and kind of hid it from everybody—even Lucky.

Anyway, Hack—poor, soft-hearted Hack—couldn't handle the disposal. He needed us to bury "poor little Scamp." So we did. We carried the box and a couple of shovels to the vacant lot and began to dig.

It was such an odd experience. Out of respect for Hack, we should have been solemn and businesslike, but for some reason, we couldn't keep from looking at each other and smiling. A couple of more shovelsful and we were chuckling. Within moments we were laughing. Nothing was funny, but we were laughing. My dad was not a man who laughed very often. So we sat down and got it out of our systems. We hoped Hack was not watching, but we knew he was not. It would have been too painful for him. Soon we got ourselves under control and began to feel rather self-conscious, avoiding each other's eyes lest we begin again.

When the grave was properly dug, we tenderly lowered Scamp into his final resting place. Our guilt inspired a bit of extra sensitivity, and we departed convinced that Scamp had a deeper, cleaner and more properly located grave than just about any cat could have hoped for, and that is what we reported to a grateful, tender-hearted Hack. He would have liked to relate some "Scamp stories," but we excused ourselves, using our farming responsibilities as our escape hatch.

Safe journey, Scamp.

><

As manager of the A&P store, Hack knew everyone in town, it seemed. He and his sister, my mother, had that quality that the rest of us so envy: everybody just naturally and immediately liked them. Had it been their nature, they could have sponged on everyone and never lifted a finger. Instead they were conscientious and industrious; in fact, overly so, most of the time.

Gordon, Hack's produce manager, came into some tickets to an L.A. Angels–Hollywood Stars baseball game at Gilmore Field, and my dad and I got invited along. Free tickets to Triple-A baseball was a treat indeed.

To Hack and Gordon, a baseball game was a beer bust with athletic entertainment included. They really liked beer! My dad drank one now and then, but he didn't belong in the same beer-drinking ballpark with Hack and Gordon. They were in a league of their own.

We had box seats! Wow! This was great. We had the whole box to ourselves, and by the time the Angels took infield practice, Hack and Gordon had done some serious stadium beer drinking. They were having a good time.

The beer vendor was the busiest guy in the entire arena. There were plenty of Hack and Gordon counterparts in the stands. It was a hot day, not that it mattered, so beer sales were brisk, to say the least.

With everything as scarce as it was during the war, I wondered how beer seemed to have escaped. The breweries must have cranked up production to match Lockheed and Douglas. I thought Hack and Gordon alone could cause a shortage.

Anyway, along about the fourth inning, Gordon signaled the popular beer vendor and lined up three full paper cups of beer on the ledge of our box. Turning to extract his wallet from his hip pocket, he brushed all three foaming containers just enough to send them over the side and directly onto the occupants of the box in front of and slightly below us. The three cups became a sudsy, yellow cascade of seeming tidal wave proportion, drenching the previously enthusiastic baseball fans below like a tsunami in a DeMille epic.

When the disaster struck, the victims reacted quickly, but not quickly enough. There was no escape route. They bumped into each other and off the walls. The beer followed them with a mind of its own, and at the conclusion of the confusion, they were soaked as if their private box had been a doomed submarine in a sea of Falstaff beer.

Confusion began to be replaced by anger, and the anger began to expand as the beer-soaked victims became aware that Gordon could not help laughing. It *was* funny, but only to the spectators. Personally, I was nervous, and I wanted Gordon to stop laughing.

Some serious name-calling began to emanate from the foamy box, and Gordon began to realize that these guys didn't take a joke very well—even an accidental joke. Gordon's nature, to laugh at everything, had gotten him in trouble before. He was not the type to do combat, but his reaction was always in advance of his common sense.

My uncle, of course, would be of no use in a fracas whatsoever, and that left, of course, my dad, perhaps a bit over-qualified, overly receptive.

No stranger to stormy situations, my dad took the prominent position, moving the rest of us back—not out of harm's way—just out of the way. If the situation did not quickly subside, he didn't want to worry about us.

Hack made certain that Gordon stayed out of the way and quiet. He was knowledgeable relative to my dad's capabilities in situations which called for forceful, physical action, and we all knew things were reaching a crescendo rapidly.

I can only guess that my dad could, with a stance and a steady gaze, convince people that great peril awaited him who ignored the tacit warning he mysteriously conveyed. The message was "tough"— very tough—like a stick of dynamite with a danger sign attached. The message continued: "Don't be dumb; it could be disastrous. You *will* be hurt."

We all watched the message reach its audience, and at just the proper moment, my dad reached back for Gordon, delivered him forward, his evil eye sending another message which Gordon read loud and clear. Gordon offered up his apology and further offered to buy beers for everyone.

The hostility melted away as I watched. Gordon's natural good nature was infectious when given an opportunity to be exhibited and perceived. My dad had provided the format for this to occur, and from all appearances, things had turned around.

Now Hack introduced himself to the beer-soaked quartet and the peace treaty was signed, sealed, and delivered. Like everyone else, they thought Hack was the nicest guy they had ever met five minutes after they met him.

My dad faded into the background and let the personality boys take over—Hack, everybody's pal, and Gordon, a man with a joke a minute.

So there it was, an example of cooperative diplomacy in action— illustrated by three different approaches. At first it had seemed like my dad was the key player, but by the end of the scenario, each had contributed rather equally to the final outcome, and on the way home, as the incident was being rehashed, I was aware that each participant envied the talent and personality of the others.

If there was a top billing, it probably belonged to Hack, who through no effort at all, had inserted his influence into the inflammatory situation. His was the lasting impression left on the "beer box" occupants. He was the one they would all remember: "That nice guy, Hack."

☒

When word arrived from Minnesota that my dad's mother had died, he didn't cry, but I did. I just thought it had to be his worst day ever, but I had mistaken my family relationship for his. He was sad, but completely under control.

I had never met my dad's mother. In fact, I had never met any of my dad's family. He was the fourth son among seven boys; three sisters were interspersed in the total ten, not counting miscarriages and stillborns. He alone had left Minnesota; the entire remaining clan lived within a few miles of each other.

Home had not been a loving place for my dad. His dad, Jake, was big and tough and never let any of the boys believe for a moment that even collectively they were a force capable of defying him. He feared only one person—his tiny wife, Pearl—but except for that, Jake was Genghis Khan.

Through their developmental years, my dad's three older brothers had emulated their father and terrorized the younger boys. No surprise that my dad would grow up more than willing to be physical; it was a way of life!

According to his accounting, my dad had dropped out of school in the tenth grade and left home. At seventeen he was making pocket money as a volunteer prize fighter in Omaha. He told me he thought it made sense to get paid for fighting since he was getting boxed around at home and had nothing but the bruises to show for it. Times were tough and so was he.

If my dad missed anybody in Minnesota it would be his mother, not the rest of the roughneck clan that he had purposely distanced himself from, so it is surprising in retrospect that he felt any obligation to return. After all, the only one who mattered was dead.

In any case, the decision for the three of us to drive to Minneapolis was made and away we went, retracing much of the same territory in our 1938 Chevrolet that we had traversed in the little Ford coupe some five years earlier. The Chevy was a sedan, so we were considerably more comfortable. Additionally, we had no dog along this time. Lucky remained at home with Grandma Ellen, who would look after everything while we were gone.

I don't know how the gas rationing problem was dealt with. I know we were the lowest qualifiers in regard to the priority system, which left us with barely enough gas for an occasional Sunday drive, as I mentioned earlier. So somehow my dad succeeded in getting approvals. I think fellow workers at the mill chipped in gas stamps.

Once again, the trip was a solid adventure in my estimation. Never having met any of my dad's relatives, and aware that Minnesota was a hunting-and-fishing, lake-filled wonderland, my juices were flowing.

I was hoping for a duck hunting trip, not a popular pastime in California. My dad made no promises, but he committed to work on his brother Maurice, the sportsman of the Swigart clan. When my dad worked on something, it usually came to pass.

During the long drive, my dad spent a little time describing his father, Jake, a genuinely tough man. He spoke of how Jake would sneak up on one of the boys and surprise him with a well-placed kick to the backside that would literally lift him off the ground. Tough, hard, intimidating. Both resentment and grudging admiration were evident as he created Jake's image for us.

We wasted no time, my dad remaining at the wheel, determined to set some kind of time and endurance record. My mother and I endured as well, crossing and recrossing our legs as we tried to ignore the messages from our bladders. We stopped for gas, food, and exhaustion, nothing else.

After an eternity of abstinence from any liquids, we arrived at the farm home of my Uncle Herschel, my father's eldest brother. The scene was somewhat like a minor riot. All the Swigarts were there, and as I was to learn, that was a dangerous situation.

Six of the seven boys were present. Vernon was in the Army in Europe. Mervin, the youngest son, was in the Army as well, but he was, by reason of Pearl's death, home on leave. All three girls were in attendance, as were some six or seven cousins I never knew existed. Wives and husbands rounded out a motley group.

The dominant feature of all this was my Grandfather Jake. He walked with a limp and eased the strain on his bad leg with a cane. He was the largest person in the room. He hardly acknowledged my father as he made his way to where I stood. He stood peering down at me and he seemed to be twenty feet tall. It occurred to me that I wasn't much to see; at least I sure felt that way.

I met Jake's gaze; our eyes locked on one another for a long moment with everyone watching. I realize now that he mistook my fascination for strength. Actually, I was like a deer, frozen in fright by the unexpected glare of headlights. Finally he offered a gigantic hand and said, "I'm your grandpa, Jake."

What was going on here was an evaluation. What kind of a kid grew up in California? The question had everyone in the room curious and fascinated.

My hand had disappeared in Grandpa Jake's. I felt like I was shrinking, but I had really wanted to meet him and I blurted, "Hi, Grandpa. Are you as tough as my dad says you are?"

There was a long moment of silence before everyone in the room cracked up, and Jake, my hand still in his, broke into a huge smile. I had won Jake over, and that was definitely the key to acceptance by the clan. I was in, but the initiation was yet to come. I had unwittingly massaged Jake's ego in front of everyone. Pure luck!

✶

I had been growing up in a kitchen with a home wrapped around it, but this was something else. The farm meals were huge—all of them. Breakfast was as large as dinner and lunch was bigger than either. These people ate like every meal was their last—meat and potatoes in mountainous quantities.

The food had its effect too. Herschel's family was noticeably larger than the rest, in girth that is. Herschel was the only farmer in the family.

Everyone was glad to see my dad and meet my mother. Dad was not nearly so enthusiastic about seeing all the Swigarts again. Most of them were rather serious, especially my dad's older brothers. My dad was a bit less so, but he was no stand-up comedian either.

The exceptions were Mervin, the baby of the family, and Maurice, who had followed my father, the fifth son. They looked like Swigarts—short and powerfully built—but they were usually smiling and extroverted (somewhat out of character). I was drawn to them because they were so approachable, but I was fascinated by the older boys, because I couldn't imagine anyone bullying my dad. By his own admission, they had.

One of the brothers, Elston, had a major black eye. We were to learn that it was the end product of an altercation with brother

Orville, or Ord, as he was known to the family. My dad informed me that this was pretty standard, and that it was unlikely anyone, including the principals, would know the reason for the set-to.

My focus, though, went to Maurice. He was the key to a duck-hunting junket, and if he liked me, I figured there would be no reason for him to resist. It looked to me like Maurice liked everybody. I saw duck hunting in my future.

The kids were mostly girls. Only a couple of boys, and one was considerably older than I. The boy nearest my age was the son of one of my dad's sisters. He was quite big for his age—almost fat but not quite. When we went outside, he threw me down and sat on me. I didn't see it coming, and my efforts to move and make a contest of it went nowhere. He weighed too much. A successful sneak attack, the skirmish was over before it began.

I was more upset than I let on. The sneak attack was not the fashion among Pacific Lane kids. This was comparable to Pearl Harbor—preadolescent, but dastardly anyway.

I conceded, but I would look for an opportunity to get even. The girls had witnessed the dastardly deed and that made it worse. Surprisingly, they chided my attacker for his tactics, which only made him laugh. He let me up and it was if nothing had ever happened. Russell Carhill had established dominance and was now willing to be pals. He was bigger and stronger, but I had this feeling that I was smarter and quicker. I would wait and watch for my opportunity. He put his arm around me as we walked, and one would have thought we were best friends. I was outwardly forgiving, but I had a grudge growing within.

⚏

I was eager to look around a real farm. The kids were most willing to show me the points of interest. It was a busy place, buzzing with activity. The focal point, from the kids' perspective, was a horse, which they could hardly wait to show me.

Enroute to the stall, I described my riding abilities, which the kids accepted, but volunteered that my experience would be of no value relative to this animal. This was not a horse one rode, they informed me; he was a work horse and didn't like anyone on his back.

He was big and nasty and mean.

I was stunned when I saw him. He was gigantic! He appeared to be like five horses of the type Red and I rode. He seemed as big and strong as an elephant. These kids were obviously afraid of him—including Russ Carhill—and no wonder. I was impressed, but not afraid. Not terrified, anyway. His name was Frank, short for Frankenstein. A real monster! An idea was beginning to form in my mind.

ΞΞ

Duck hunting is an early-morning sport, I was to learn. Maurice had me up at three in the morning. He wanted to be at the lake by five. I was excited and ready in a flash, so we arrived early, a bit after four.

At the lake was not quite accurate. By four-thirty we would be *in* the lake. We had on waders, and although I had two thick layers of clothes on, I couldn't stop shaking—a combination of cold and early morning. I was freezing! Duck hunting was not what I had cracked it up to be. My chattering teeth would surely scare off the ducks, I thought.

I had a 20-gauge shotgun which was the prize possession of Maurice's wife, Dorothy. Maurice had a 12-gauge. We were ready to put a big dent in the Minnesota duck population; bring on the ducks. Maybe some action would warm us up; but the shivering and shaking surely wouldn't help my aim.

Maurice had borrowed a hunting dog from a friend. Like me, Maurice looked very uncomfortable. On the way to the lake, he advised me that duck hunting was not his favorite form of the sport. He liked to trek into Canada after deer, elk, and moose. "That," he advised, "is hunting." It sounded great to me, too. It had to be more comfortable than standing in a lake at this ungodly hour.

The dog, by contrast, was in heaven! A golden retriever-lab mix, the animal was excited enroute, but once he sighted the marsh, he was ecstatic. Looney tunes was more like it. What a retriever-lab has in its cranial cavity is a mystery. It cannot be a brain, but no matter, we all wish we could be more like them.

The dog's exuberance, while puzzling, took our minds off our discomfort to a degree, so brainless or not, I was glad he was along. My dad had a favorite little description of dog intelligence. He would say, "Most dogs have a brain about the size of a pea, but this dog has a real little one." A perfect description of this dog. He sure was happy, though.

When the first flock of ducks came over, my gun was on safety, and by the time I realized it, the ducks were long gone. Maurice had been more preoccupied with getting me into the action than getting a shot off himself, so these ducks would remain alive and safely on the wing unless there were other, more adept hunters in the area. We vowed to be ready when the next wave streaked above us.

There was no shortage of ducks in Minnesota. They came over us by the hundreds, maybe millions! I was usually only quick enough to be shooting at tail feathers. The ducks flew over at something near the speed of sound, and I was blasting away at empty airspace.

Maurice was no great marksman himself. He used up a lot of shells bringing down two ducks. Unless my technique improved, I would have no pangs of guilt this night. I had killed nothing. It was impossible for the damned things to escape the spray of shot that I would direct at them, but they did. If you point the gun at something and pull the trigger, the rest was supposed to be automatic. Tell the ducks!

Each flight would result in four blasts from our dual double barrels, and usually no birds. The dog seemed puzzled at the lack of retrieving, splashing around expectantly but finding little retriever duty to perform. He clearly expected ducks to be in the water.

Finally all the 20-gauge shells were gone. They had resulted in zero kills. Maurice still had a few 12-gauge shells left, so he turned the big gun over to me with a perfunctory warning that it would kick harder than the 20-gauge. "So be prepared," he suggested.

I wasn't prepared! In the excitement of the low-flying comets, I failed to seat the butt of the gun into my shoulder, and when I pulled the trigger, the surprise force of the recoil caused me to pull the second trigger. In quick succession, I went from staggering backwards to landing on the seat of my pants in knee-deep, near-freezing water. I was now chest deep; waders were of no value here. The great duck hunting trip was over, as my layered clothing soaked up the lake.

Maurice thought it was really funny, but he had seen many a novice humiliated by a double blast from a 12-gauge shotgun, so it did not brand me as a sissy or anything like that. In fact, to my knowledge, he never told that part of the story to anyone, which qualified him as a pretty darned nice guy in my opinion. On the way home, we talked about our lack of skill and laughed at our ineptitude. It was the best part of the day, and we were glad we had shared an adventure, even one so unsuccessful. Maurice was really a nice guy, I thought.

✖

I made a point of stealing away for a few moments whenever I could during the next few days. Armed with a treat for Frank, I spent the time introducing myself and seeking his acceptance. He was a bit suspicious and skittish, but I hung in, careful not to get in a position where his huge bulk could make a pancake out of me.

It took only a few visits to notice a difference. I didn't have Red's mystic way with horses, but I had a little of the quality. It was mainly a combination of my love for animals and my lack of fear, I guess. In any case, it was working with Frank, I could tell. We were getting comfortable with each other. It was unlikely he had been treated with my kind of gentleness, and I suspect my size might have served to my advantage. It was obvious he had little to fear from me.

I had been very leery of Russ Carhill since the "sneak attack" took place. I had expected more bullyish behavior, but to my surprise, nothing of that nature had taken place. Even more surprising was the fact that I couldn't stay mad at him. Since that first incident, he had been friendly and gone out of his way to make me feel included and entertained. What was that sneak attack all about, anyway? This was a very nice guy, and we were having some good times together.

The girls had been terrific from the start. There was no gender gap. We were just kids, and I wished that all these kids could be moved to Pacific Lane. I was really enjoying myself.

✖

It was hard to tell that anyone had died. Curiosity about the Californians ran high and upstaged my grandmother's passing. We kids just didn't have the attention span to properly respect the recently deceased, but the adults were no better. Perhaps it was for the best. I hoped Grandma Pearl, whom I had never met, would approve. A little more reverence would have made me more comfortable, though.

If we stayed much longer, I would be as big as Russ Carhill. These meals were designed to make one grow, and it worked. My skinny little body was becoming fleshier almost overnight. Everyone thought that it was grand that we kids were getting along so well, having so much fun, and the skinny kid from California was gaining weight to boot.

But time had run out. The funeral was over and our visit was at an end.

Our departure day had arrived and everyone was at the farm to see us off. It was the same crowd that had greeted us on our arrival. These people were really clannish, and somehow my dad had missed out on the "clan gene"; he was ready to leave and never look back. In all honesty, I think he had grown up more than the others, and he had left the rest of them behind—cut the umbilical cord in a way they couldn't, and it fascinated them. He couldn't wait to do it again, and although it wasn't my feeling, I understood for him.

As everyone gathered outside, I slipped away to the barn. When I emerged astride the gigantic Frank, the ones that counted, the kids, Jake, and Herschel, stood in stunned amazement. Their mouths were actually open. I had command of Frank. I had been astride him before, secretly in his stall, and he was quite comfortable with me. I must have looked like a peanut on the back of an elephant. Maybe so, but I felt like John Wayne, and the important thing was Russ Carhill thought so too, I could tell. This was my sneak counterattack, and the response was at least as great as I had hoped. Russ stood with his mouth wide open, speechless.

My dad, who really didn't like horses very much and had no idea what was going on, told me to put the horse away and get in the car. "It is time to leave." My mother looked worried. I wasn't too sure I could get Frank to go back to his stall. Majestically, the huge horse obeyed my commands and we reentered the barn, to my great relief.

I slipped off the horse, using the side of the stall for a ladder in the same manner I had mounted, and took the bridle off. Jake and Hersch were there to meet me, and we walked out of the barn together. The patriarch and eldest brother and me—I felt like General MacArthur!

Jake shook my hand in a special gesture of goodbye. Hersch took the time to tell me that he had expected a sissy from California, but was happy to find that I was a real "regular kid," and I should come back to visit the farm again one day. He said he about had a heart attack when he saw me on Frank.

It was the kind of recognition Russ Carhill dreamed of and, I realized, the reason for the sneak attack. Another incident in his search for acceptance from a tough audience. I hoped Russ would discover that he was a terrific kid and not worry so much about impressing everybody all the time. It wouldn't be easy though. I couldn't really imagine where, among all those critical, judgmental people constantly evaluating everyone, any serious sensitivity would come from. Russ would have to learn to satisfy himself about himself. There were sure to be more sneak attacks in Russ's future, I feared.

During the trip home my dad seemed very different than he had been enroute to Minnesota. It was more than just relief to have it over with. I think it confirmed for him the direction he had chosen to follow. He alone among all his siblings had reached out. He seemed a bit proud of himself, and I admired him, too. He exhibited a strength the others couldn't match, hence their great curiosity during our stay. His strength was more than just physical. It didn't hurt that his kind of skinny, city-raised kid had fared okay, either. He was feeling pretty good, we could tell. So was I.

We couldn't waste any time returning home. My dad and mother both needed to return to their jobs, and I was due back in school. My dad would never admit he was tired. He drove until our protests would finally succeed in getting him to stop. The trip home seemed long, as my mother and I sang together to pass the hours.

✄

Playing in the band and marching while playing were two different things, and required skills I hadn't acquired. I don't mean walking and playing; that I could handle. Staying in step was a bit more demanding, but Mr. Sauter required more. He wanted us to form a block letter "T" while playing the fight song, and I found myself at some real disadvantages. I was accustomed to being the smallest person in the band, and that of course meant I had the shortest legs. So when things really began to move, while others lengthened their stride, I was required to break into a trot. When they broke into a trot, I was in full flight. This was hopeless, but the goal was glorious, and I wanted my place in the "T" even if I looked foolish in the process. Woodwind instruments are not designed to be played on a dead run.

To be out there where the gladiators vied—the grandstands filled with admirers, me dressed in satin maroon-and-gray cape and cap, playing "Fight on, for Torrance High" while the entire student body sang along with all the gusto they could muster—was a thrill. As the "T" materialized from some thirty antlike, scrambling musicians, the crowd would cheer madly, and they would be cheering what I had helped create: the "T." I had to be a part of it. I just had to keep up.

I felt like I was in a musical game of crack the whip. Benny Goodman couldn't play clarinet on a dead run; how the hell could I? All I could do was try my best, but after I went spinning out of control a couple of times, I knew Mr. Sauter was becoming aware of a problem with his precision marching band. He positioned himself up in the grandstand, high enough to see everything, and I had my old sinking feeling spreading in all directions from a spot deep in my stomach. My band career was in deep jeopardy, I just knew it.

I arrived at my appointed position in the "T" about three steps and five notes late. Mr. Sauter left us in place as he descended from his all-seeing lofty perch where no amount of effort on my part could have disguised the problem. I was dead meat! It wasn't fair, this discrimination against small people. People with short legs have feelings too, and some of them are better clarinet players than people with long legs, I thought. It was a speech I knew I would never deliver, so I braced myself for the bad news as well as the humiliation. My "washing-out ceremony" would take place in the presence of the entire band.

Mr. Sauter summoned me to him and my face flushed crimson as the sweat popped out all over my body. My feet moved me along to where he was standing without any signal from my brain, which was racing in an attempt to locate some route of escape, while knowing there was none. Before I could reach him, Mr. Sauter ordered me to follow him to a spot in the precise center of the field. Would my court martial be so formal, I wondered?

"This," he said, "is where I want you to stand. March straight to this spot."

Could I be dreaming? I was not dismissed, defrocked (of my cape and cap) and discarded as I had expected. In fact, Mr. Sauter had solved my problem and his by making me the center of the universe. I was the pointman of the "T." The entire activity would form around me. I was the nucleus of the Torrance High School Marching Band and the glorious block letter "T."

A couple more rehearsals confirmed that we would look great on game day. The "T" seemed to form as if by magic, or so it seemed to me. The people in the stands were going to be so impressed. I was really glad I had learned to play the clarinet. This is surely the kind of stuff that impresses girls. Now where did that thought come from? Only a moment ago I thought I was a goner; now I'm a hero with girls on my mind. Life is confusing, I thought. It wouldn't have taken a psychologist to figure it out.

The only thing the large near-adult males in the band talked about was girls. I had expected more talk about music. The main subcategory was anatomy (i.e., "Norma has great boobs"; "Virginia has great legs"; "Dorothy has a great ass"). These conversations were running ahead of my emotional capacity. I had fantasies of putting my arm around a girl or holding hands. These people sometimes talked about the most intimate female body parts, in great detail. It made me feel self-conscious, but it also got me thinking. These thoughts would have been better off in the mind of one a bit more mature and better equipped emotionally to understand and cope with them, but there I was, in the wave, even though this wave had too much water!

✄

The best musician in the band was a trumpet player. This was a bit of a disappointment. Reed players are not great admirers of the brass section. But the overriding emotion was surprise—surprise because most high school trumpet players concentrated more on volume than quality. They just seemed to think the idea was to drown everyone else out, and they usually did. Mr. Sauter had his hands full trying to get feeling instead of volume from the brass.

Harry James was the master of trumpet, but teenage trumpet players had nothing in common with him. That is, none but Moe Jarrett.

The sounds that Moe produced were so sweet, so pure, that I simply couldn't get enough. His talent went beyond tone; he didn't make mistakes, either. All of the rest of us made mistakes. Our attention spans were poor, our concentration drifted, and when one is attempting to coordinate what the sheet music is conveying to the eye, the eye to the brain, the brain to the hands, the hands to the fingers, the lungs to the lips, the lips to the reed—concentration is essential, else you settle for something less than music in the form intended. Most of us settled.

When the subject is music, perfection is the only acceptable level. One flaw destroys the entire product. By definition it must be perfect. At the high school level, perfection rarely lasts long.

Moe was so much better than the rest of us, I wondered why, and I wondered if I could hope to be so good one day. Moe was two years older than I; could that be the reason? I knew better. There were many band members his age, but none sounded like he did. Age was not the secret. Intuitively I knew that if I asked Mr. Sauter, he would credit the great span between Moe and the rest of us to practice—specifically practice scales. Ugh! He never stopped pleading with us to practice, and we gave it our own interpretive spin. If we could find the time, we would. We rarely found much time.

There was really nothing to lose by asking Mr. Sauter, even if my guess was right. I did, and it was! Mr. Sauter seized the opportunity and attempted to turn practice into a religious experience, capable of producing miracles.

I listened and nodded appropriately, but because the response had been predictable, little of it really sank in. Too simple, I thought. There was a secret, and I wanted to know what it was.

I didn't know Moe, had never spoken to him, and to ask him directly was not so simple. I didn't want to seem foolish or worse, young, but I needed to know the secret of Moe's superior musical abilities, and it really only made sense to hear it from him.

✕

Ralph, the flute player who sat next to me, was great fun—a gentle giant who was always in a good mood, joking and acting funny. He thought it was great fun to reverse the beginning letters of words. Mr. Sauter, for example, became "Sister Mauter." Moe Jarrett became "Joe Marrett." It was silly, but I would laugh till my sides hurt. He "flayed the plute" and Moe "trayed the plumpet." When we got to Phyllis Tucker, it was too much. Mr. Sauter asked us to share the hysterics with the rest, but instead of waiting, tapped his baton and we dutifully got ourselves together. The baton wielded more power than a flame thrower. I avoided eye contact with Ralph so it wouldn't start all over again. You can't play the clarinet and giggle at the same time.

I decided on the direct approach with Moe Jarrett. I simply asked him how much he practiced. Sadly, I learned once again that my quest to find just one thing at which I could excel by shortcut—discovering a secret passageway to success—was to end in the usual fashion. Was there never to be a substitute for hard work?

Moe walked around with a trumpet mouthpiece in his hand all the time. He told me that when he wasn't practicing he was playing trumpet in his mind. He ate, slept and dreamed trumpet. He practiced *scales!* I couldn't fathom the dedication required to practice scales. He was explaining to me and advising me of the joy of practice. I made a mental note to admire Moe from a distance in the future and to reevaluate my musical objectives. Scales, Jesus!

✕

Our visit to the Swigart clan was apparently misinterpreted as a friendly overture by my dad's brothers and sisters. Letters began to arrive indicating that when the war ended and gas rationing ended, we could expect visits from the midwest. My dad did not express pleasure. The letters went unanswered.

✕

I was in high school now—the seventh grade. I had the advantage of knowing some people and knowing my way around. My disadvantage, the main one anyway, was my inability to grow any body hair prior to my entry into the hostile territory known as the "boys' gym." I had no underarm hair and no pubic hair. No hair anywhere but on my head. It was not a comfortable situation.

There were guys who had hair that started at their belly button and disappeared into their Levis—the uniform at Torrance High for the boys, Levis and white T-shirts. There were guys whose underarm hair came down below the rolled up short sleeve of the shirt. Since gym classes had a mix of people in each class, some of these hairy people were in every class.

It was like showering with one's father and his friends. My seventh-grade classmates and I used our towels for fig leaves (a rose petal would have covered what we were hiding) and tried to present our backsides when actually showering. Some would say nudity is the great equalizer, but not when one is a seventh grader and another a senior. It was really humiliating. I would inspect my body nightly for any sign of an emerging hair.

At least I had memorized my locker combinations and felt pretty secure about avoiding swats, but the gym atmosphere was really intimidating. The upper-class guys wore anything they wanted. Most of them were off-season athletes, required to be in a physical education class, but it was only for the record. They just amused themselves while we lined up dutifully in our gray shorts and T-shirts, a combination seemingly designed to make us appear insignificant and hopeless, athletically.

The coaches were sadistic martinets by nature. It was their genetic destiny to make us feel intimidated. They loved their athletes and felt that someone else should really have to deal with these tiny little children. It was clear that they despised us.

I prayed there would be no rain, in case there was some truth about the dancing and the foot kissing. It could happen, I thought to myself.

What made things worse was the fact that a few—not many, but a few—kids our age *were* hairy already. Not fair, was my reaction to that. In high school, one *needed* body hair. Why wasn't it automatic?

So every day in gym class I found myself experiencing a feeling much like the "egg behind the keg." What was wrong with my body hair? Why wouldn't it sprout somewhere? Give me a sign that my next six years of school wouldn't find me holding a towel to cover my hairless, exposed, underdeveloped little male stuff. There must be something I could rub on myself, I thought, but if there were, my dad would have been rubbing it on his head. His increasing baldness was driving him crazy. Nevertheless, I would check the ads in any magazine I could get my hands on. Maybe I needed some hormones.

Entering high school at the seventh-grade level at twelve or thirteen years of age was especially hard. There were more problems than I have time to relate, but a couple of things illustrate why it was so difficult, even though we were excited to be there.

For starters, as I mentioned, we were just too young. The seniors were four to six years older than we were, and at our age it represented a full one third of our existence on earth. They were adults and we were little kids. The same span existed in grammar school, but the oldest kids there were not adults, they were still just kids. It was not the same, not even remotely. I went around feeling like I might get stepped on by some gigantic person who would fail to see me in time.

Our first day was an ordeal, but getting lipstick smeared all over our faces was traditional, and we "scrubs" were long since clued in, so we endured—knowing we would look foolish, but also knowing that the movie star-like senior boys had once looked similarly foolish. It was a comforting thought.

Much more serious was the fact that we weren't quite sure where we were supposed to be at any given time, and we had a disproportionate fear of the penalty for getting there late. Once there, the reception was nothing like what we were accustomed to in grammar school. In our previous lives, we were, by comparison, embraced, guided, shown, encouraged, and led. Enter Mrs. Burnham!

Mrs. Burnham was the designated "Top Sergeant" at Torrance High School. We had no way of knowing her stern, scowling, hardline attitude was part of the program designed to mold our study habits, which required self-discipline to replace the coddling and prodding that typified the grammar school system.

She had me terrified!

Usually my assignments waited until the last minute before the due date, but when Mrs. Burnham announced that we were to memorize "The quality of mercy" from *The Merchant of Venice*, I began immediately. I wanted no part of Mrs. Burnham's acerbic commentary she reserved for those who dallied. (Yes, I would have been better off had more of my teachers been like Mrs. Burnham.)

The desks in her class had inkwells, and we were given black wooden pens with replaceable tips. We were expected to write with them, a really impossible task. The downstroke was okay, but the upstroke invariably dug into the cheap, soft paper, spreading droplets of ink, totally indelible, over a square inch or two, where neatness was the only objective of the exercise.

The inkwell was an accident waiting for a catalytic seventh-grader to do something clumsy. Everything I did was clumsy.

For some unknown reason the tiny reservoir of ink was just too enticing to ignore, and the slightest tampering produced a chain reaction that could not be stopped until it had resulted in the maximum damage it could cause. Once the ink was released, it sought to get on everything. Attempts to stop or somehow reverse the process merely created a new direction for the insidious liquid to turn, always seeking the lightest hue with which to merge.

I found myself involved in this hopeless situation, panic rising as I tried to corral the black glop, which was out of its cage as if alive, refusing to be recaptured.

The girl in front of me already had ink on her previously milk-white sweater; I had ink on both hands and elbows, while rivulets were forming on the desktop, whose gentle slope invited gravity to express itself.

Mrs. Burnham, the martinet disguised as an English literature teacher, was addressing the class, but my mind was occupied. What she was saying was bound to be important in the near future, but I could deal with only one death struggle at a time. Ink, it appeared, had the capability of ending a high school career in a single incident.

I had nothing with which to blot the spreading fluid, which was now dripping onto the crotch of my yellowish cords. At last something was absorbing the relentless flow of the black tidal wave.

To have leaped out of the way would have resulted in discovery, so I allowed the ink to spread in as many dimensions as existed: inward, outward, upward and downward. I felt it pass through my shorts.

This was a serious inkstain we're talking about. My hand was not large enough to conceal it, and how would that look, anyway?

Confession had not occurred to me as a viable option. I imagined the salvo of Burnham rage that would surely be unleashed; this was the incident she had trained for.

Why couldn't the ink have been acid and just dissolved me?

The desktops in Mrs. Burnham's classroom, unlike those in other classrooms, were pristine. No one dared write or carve on one of her desks. One desk had lost its perfect complexion—mine!

The moment of truth was imminent. Soon I would be staring directly into the eyes of death, for to add to the urgency of my inky disaster, the bell ending the Burnham hour was only a few ticks away.

When it came, my eyes closed and my head rolled back; the room emptied like a flushed toilet—I alone remained.

Mrs. Burnham was not accustomed to anyone remaining in her class after the bell rang. She must have thought I was unconscious. She began to close the distance between us, and my heart started to race, perspiration popped out on my forehead and I felt lightheaded. I hoped I would faint; no such luck. She reached my desk and looked down at me. Her eyes moved across the inkstained desktop and came to rest on the spent reservoir. I watched as her neck turned red, and like the ink on my cords, the color seeped upward to her face. She had her most menacing gaze fixed on me now.

An eternity passed, and I felt something squeeze my throat from the inside—I was going to be seriously sick, and I didn't think I would be able to breathe much longer. I looked down at my book, *The Merchant of Venice,* and to this day I'll never know if what happened was a conscious thought, a spontaneous reaction, or a miracle, but from some distant place I heard my voice say, "The quality of mercy is not strained, it droppeth as the gentle rain from heaven upon the place beneath; it is twice blest; it blesseth him that gives, and him that takes."

Her expression changed, softened. I watched her rage melt away as I continued through the entire appeal. At the finish I saw my first Burnham smile ever. Had it ever been seen before—by anybody? For the first time I felt there would be no demand for a pound of my flesh.

Very softly she said "Bravo." And then she collected herself, crossed her arms across her stout, buxom chest and asked me what I was going to do about the defiled desk.

I would live, perhaps even graduate from high school someday.

That's the way I wished it had happened, but alas, the truth is I snuck out with the crush of departing students, hiding the inkstain behind the bard's works.

Desks had not been assigned, so the following day I simply assumed a different location and tried to appear as innocent as possible while Mrs. Burnham unleashed a scathing indictment of the guilty coward who had committed the act of vandalism.

I endured. My heart was heavy, but more courage was required to confess than I could muster. The crime has remained an unsolved mystery until this very moment.

∞

The Columbia Steel whistle blew at 8:00 a.m. and 4:30 p.m. It could be heard throughout the entire town and beyond. It was part of the town.

If someone was badly injured, or if there was some emergency, the whistle blew short bursts for two or three minutes, which seemed like hours. The whole town stopped what it was doing and hoped no one they knew was injured or hurt. It was exactly like the mining towns of the east except in degree. There was never anything like a cave-in at Columbia Steel. But a large percentage of the male population of Torrance worked at the mill, so anxieties soared when the whistle sounded. There was a brotherhood among the mill workers. It was not really possible to like everyone, of course, but any injured worker was top priority with all the fellow workers.

It was really quite amazing that there weren't more serious incidents; steel and flesh match up poorly, and steel wins every time. Everything there was hard, sharp, and often hot.

Columbia Steel never closed. Shift workers kept the mill running twenty-four hours a day, so when the whistle blew, more workers were off-site than on. Many of these off-duty workers would drop everything and head for the mill when the whistle blew, anxious to learn if a friend was the reason for the alarm. Friend or not, they would almost surely know the person involved. We could hardly imagine life without the 8:00 a.m. and 4:30 p.m. whistles, but we could sure live without those emergency blasts.

It was Saturday, and my dad and I were eating lunch. My grandmother had made me a fried Spam sandwich, a glass of milk, and a saucer full of "ice box" cookies. My dad was eating his usual lunch—cold cereal and coffee which he drank from a restaurant-style cup that was so thick it really didn't hold much liquid. The coffee it did hold was insulated. It remained scalding. That was the important thing. He could always refill the cup, but it was essential that the coffee be hot enough to boil the tongue of an ordinary person. Perfect for my dad.

Oddly, when the whistle began to make its short blasts, I recalled that I had been singing when I came to the breakfast table in the morning, and my grandmother had said, "Sing before breakfast, cry before night," but since my dad was here and not possibly the reason for the whistle, I relaxed. Still, I wished I hadn't thought of that.

I relaxed but my dad didn't. He leaped up, grabbed his mill cap, and was on his way. If someone was needed to help move or lift something, few were more qualified. Did he really want to help, or show off his strength, I wondered? A bit of both was my guess.

It was too far to run, too close to drive. He would walk as fast as he could and break into an occasional trot. I would have gone with him, but there was no point in it. I couldn't go inside, and I could wait outside for hours. I would get a report when he returned.

While he was gone the whistle blew again, and those damned words of my grandmother popped instantly into my head again. Almost simultaneously there was trouble in my stomach and sweat popped out on my upper lip.

I took a deep breath and tried to think logically. The odds against my dad being the cause of the alarm were long, very long. That was the correct focus for this situation. I knew it, but I couldn't get it to work. My skin was clammy and I felt a little bit dizzy. Times like these called for the assurance of a mom, and that's where I headed. I had been in the middle of chores—the damned chickens could wait.

My mother and grandmother were in the kitchen, busy with evening meal plans. They hadn't been concerned until they saw me. They thought I was sick; I must have looked like hell.

I became both the gasoline and the match when I related my sense of doom—this inescapable feeling that the whistle was for my dad. Everybody has a bit of superstition in him, and I had rubbed the lamp and let the genie out. In no time the ladies were as concerned as I was—a minor step short of panic. The power of suggestion was being graphically illustrated.

We became emotional Keystone Cops. Our feelings bounced around and gained momentum in the process. We were irrational but couldn't reach back for the logic drifting in the wake of our rising panic.

My mother was frantically trying to call the mill for information, but never having done that before, she was making little progress and becoming more frightened and frustrated by the minute.

Suddenly my dad was in the room. He had come into the kitchen unnoticed because we were so distracted, and for a moment we just stood staring, as if we were seeing a ghost. He had a strange expression on his face which added to the oddness of the moment.

Our emotions were experiencing a violent U-turn as we tried to hang on. We converged on my dad—not a common thing around our house. Overt displays of emotion were not consistent with his general behavior, or ours either, for that matter. He was obviously puzzled by the reception, and his somber reaction to our euphoria began to have a sobering effect on us. He had something on his mind.

We pulled ourselves together and told him that we had been worried about him, but he hardly heard us. He had arrived on the accident scene to find that one of his closest mates had been dreadfully injured when a cable which had been delivering a bundle of steel bars used in construction had snapped and spilled its contents. The bars were no problem, but the cable had been under great stress and had whipped through the air like a long, slender rapier. It had taken his friend's leg off at the knee faster than the eye could follow.

When my dad arrived, his mate was going into shock. Before anyone could do much about it, the man's heart had stopped beating. My father had arrived in time to witness his passing, and the unreal quality of the event had not fully penetrated as yet, but I was feeling very grateful that it hadn't been my dad.

Tears welled in my dad's eyes and my mood changed instantly, as I realized how affected my dad was by the loss of a friend.

Somewhere in Torrance, in another kitchen, a sad scene was taking place. That which we had imagined had become reality for the family of the dead mill worker, and my dad was suffering from just a sip, just the tiniest taste of what they would be feeling. The worst of it for him was that all his strength, his willingness, and readiness were useless, and he had been helpless to do anything to save his friend.

The first whistle had signaled an injury; the second had been sounded by an employee feeling much as my dad felt: frustrated and defeated.

I collapsed into bed early that evening. I was drained—glad my dad was okay but unable to escape the guilt that accompanied my happiness about it.

Life is very complicated. My dad worked in a very dangerous place. I hoped the whistle would never sound again except at 8:00 a.m. and 4:30 p.m.

✂

For just a moment I thought hair had miraculously grown under my arms, but closer inspection revealed lint from my dark woolen shirt had been left there, fused to my skin by dried sweat. My disappointment and my vigil would continue.

There were other frustrating mysteries. Why was I so small and skinny? My dad was short, but muscular and powerful-appearing. Why was it taking so long for me to take on my dad's physical characteristics?

When it finally happened, I would be one very popular high schooler. I was convinced I would see the signs any day. All that stood between me and popularity with the girls was height, weight, body hair, and muscles. As I thought about it though, that still might not be enough. Girls are just so mysterious. Who knows what they want? The only girls I really knew were in my class, but they had little interest in the boys in my class—especially me, it seemed.

Older boys *were* interested and so were our girls. Our female population was being stolen away from us—even Richard Bayless was ineffective. Marie had moved on. A guy two grades higher, whom I had seen in the shower, was circling her. He looked older than Gregory Peck to me, and hairier! I made a mental note to be ready to get a girlfriend when next year's crop arrived.

Most of the boys like myself were left as if on a desert island. There were no girls younger than we were in our school. We represented the bottom rung on the ladder of "boy meets girl." So we generally just resigned ourselves to developing sports skills and began some solitary experimentation. Our inferiority complexes were about to be complicated with some genuine sexual guilt. We knew we shouldn't be doing those things, or thinking these nasty, dirty things, but there was no avoiding sex, once discovered.

The word "sex" hardly existed in oral form. It was more secret and mysterious than the Japanese military code. Like being dropped in the middle of a mine field, there was no help. One either found one's way through it alone or one exploded into tiny pieces—in one's bathroom, frequently.

Try as I might to control myself, my secret bathroom meetings with Sheena, Queen of the Jungle, were becoming more and more frequent. I knew I was betraying my mother with each episode and couldn't escape the feeling that she was watching the entire disgusting spectacle; but God, it felt so good. I was doing something terribly wrong, so vile and so forbidden that I couldn't confide in anyone. I honestly did not know if anyone else did it or not. Resistance was futile. In fact, the intervals between episodes seemed to be narrowing at warp speed. At this rate I was in jeopardy of ultimately spending my life locked in the bathroom.

I thought it was supposed to be fun to be a kid. Why did it seem like I was always facing some new ordeal? Some trapdoor was always swallowing me and dumping me into a terrifying, unfamiliar place, with no escape available unless I agonizingly stumbled around and by some stroke of luck, that provided no key to future escape routes, was deposited once again safely on the beach. I would still be feeling exposed, humiliated, and defenseless, unable to avoid being swept away once again by the next unexpected overpowering wave.

✖

The guys in the band were talking again, and the subject was always the same and not what I needed to hear. Quite often the specific individual under discussion was an attractive junior girl named Jean Sparks. Ah, the fair Jean Sparks.

If one believed all the talk, Jean was the relief valve for a lot of pressure building in a lot of young male musicians. I was a male musician, I reminded myself, and perhaps experiencing the real thing would cure me of my addiction to my bathroom relief valve. Could there be, I wondered, time in Jean's busy sexual schedule for me? And if so, how to get things moving? There was a huge gap between these initial questions and a successful conclusion, no doubt about that. Was there even a chance?

Suppressing my confidence, among other things, was this problem of body hair. If I needed it to feel comfortable in the gym shower, I was sure as hell going to need it in this ultimate intimacy. (We would be naked, wouldn't we?) I had this sinking thought that this stuff I was doing in the bathroom was inhibiting the maturation of my body. Was this guilt or a discovery? If I had hit upon the cause, I would *never* have any body hair at this rate.

Another major problem: If I succeeded in my quest to actually couple with Jean Sparks, I did not want to produce a baby in the process, and I felt quite certain she would feel the same. I would need a rubber. How would I ever get a rubber?

Looking back, life seemed so simple when I thought about airplanes instead of girls. So think about airplanes, I tried to tell myself, with a feeling of futility.

✖

I had anticipated that when pubic hair finally appeared it would emerge one hair at a time, in kind of random fashion—perhaps one in the middle, then on the right, then left and so on. So it was to my great surprise, not to mention delight, that one day traces appeared—multiples of fleecy hairs that would eventually exhibit some of the properties of Bermuda grass. It was fascinating—so fascinating that I was drawn to examine myself a lot, which only led to more bathroom romances. Elation blended with guilt, a bad combination.

But at last it had happened. I would almost surely grow into a normal adult male. Perhaps I would even possess some undefinable animal magnetism, some irresistible quality that females could not resist. God! Body hair was wonderful!

✖

I really thought I wanted to be a Boy Scout. I had been a Cub Scout and had done okay, although my mother had really walked me through most of the requirements for Wolf, Bear, and Lion. Moving on to full-fledged Boy Scouting seemed like a natural thing to do. Moe Jarrett was edging toward Eagle and it appeared to me that achieving Eagle was almost a state of grace; an Eagle was considered a perfect young person by just about everybody.

I worried that I would not be able to live up to my parents' expectations, and scouting, especially the lofty Eagle rank, looked like a way to satisfy them and let me relax a bit from the pressure I felt to always do and be better.

Was the pressure real or imagined? A bit of both. We all experienced these feelings, I'm sure.

Dick Turner was a scout and his parents were "troop parents." I liked Dick, and his parents were terrific people. The troop was growing because of them. I wanted in before there was no room for me. It wouldn't hurt to already know the principals.

There was a tiny, distant voice deep within me that seemed unconvinced, but where was the peril? Scouting had a universally positive reputation.

At twelve, everything can be explained by physiology. Most importantly the veins and arteries are getting crowded, hormones are multiplying and replacing blood, which is critical if the brain is to function. In my case, the little voices were symptomatic of impaired brain function, but unfortunately, a second symptom was the inability to recognize and react properly to the first symptom.

I joined the scouts and swore "to do my best to do my duty." I was a tenderfoot in Troop 217.

This was great! Dick Turner was already a second-class scout, and his brother, Jack, was a first-class. Their dad, "Pop" Turner, welcomed me in, and Mrs. Turner told me how happy she was to have me in the troop. She knew my mother and knew Esther's boy would be the kind of kid they wanted in 217. My mother had that effect on people.

It didn't take long for the little voice to get a little more specific. It had something to do with regimentation. It seemed to make me real nervous. I had developed, among other better known hormones, an anti-regimentation hormone, just what my brain blood supply needed.

When everyone was required to line up or do something in unison, I got sweaty palms. Scouting appeared to be more regimented the more exposure I got. Increasingly, scouts seemed kind of like robots to me.

Some scouts had uniforms and some did not. There was no stigma to wearing "civvies," but everyone wanted a uniform. I wasn't so sure about me in a uniform. The regimentation stuff again. They were expensive, but that wasn't the reason. How could a boy of twelve recognize a blood-hormone imbalance?

There would be a Fourth of July parade, and while we got no pressure to be in uniform from Pop or Mrs. Turner, we all wanted to march proudly through town looking as genuine as possible. It was the reason we needed to become uniformly uniformed.

My parents were willing to pay. They were delighted with the entire program, especially since the Turners were highly respected people in the community. Scouting was wholesome, and my mother liked wholesome. Besides, I had successfully completed the rather simple requirements to attain second-class. I was a Tenderfoot no more. This success suggested, we thought, the likelihood that I would be a good Boy Scout and that the investment in a uniform would not be wasted.

J.C. Penney Company was scout supply headquarters in Torrance. My mother had arranged for me to pick out what I needed—a complete scout uniform, including official pocket knife, flashlight, and canteen. But something was going on, and the blood-brain situation was not in balance. The more I thought about myself in a uniform, the less attractive the idea seemed to me. Being dressed like everyone else, marching in step, robotlike, I was getting a panicky feeling before I even entered the store. I convinced myself it wouldn't hurt to look the stuff over; maybe I would like myself in a uniform once I had it on. Keep an open mind, I told myself.

I looked at everything!

I had a twofold problem. First, this growing feeling about regimentation, scout clones, robots. I felt like someone was trying to remove my face and replace it with an unidentifiable, featureless one.

Second, I knew the value of money, and since my parents wanted to finance this stuff, I wanted to be really responsible about the shopping and purchase. I intended to satisfy both criteria.

As I searched through the stacks of shirts, pants, socks, neckerchiefs, and hats, my eyes caught a section apart from the rest. One look and I knew I had found my parade day uniform.

ⅨⅨ

I had saved my scout uniform for parade day. It hadn't been ready for wear anyway, requiring the various insignia to be sewn on and some minor adjustments for proper fit.

My parents had looked a bit skeptical when they saw my purchases on display for their approval, but my enthusiasm had smothered any criticism they might have offered.

So the big day arrived, and everything fit perfectly. As I inspected myself in the mirror, I thought I looked like as impressive a scout as I had ever seen, and I didn't think I looked like every other scout in America, either, which made me comfortable.

The little voices were mercifully quiet. I would have judged that blood and hormones were bathing my brain in proper proportion. I had this scouting thing under control, and I was dealing with this developing regimentation problem quite nicely, it seemed to me.

My thought was to walk to the Turners' house and then walk to the parade area with Dick and Jack. The sun was shining, and I felt really proud and impressive as I walked the mile in the opposite direction from the parade area.

People were noticing me, I could tell. There were smiles of appreciation, and I was looking forward to the parade and the exposure that I would receive. The streets would be lined with people, including many of my classmates. There would be some impressed girls, I was sure about that. Scouting was a bonanza. I was only a second-class scout and I felt like a celebrity. I smiled back at the smiling appreciators.

I rang the doorbell and waited for a response. It required a second push of the button before Mrs. Turner appeared in the doorway. Her expression puzzled me. She definitely looked surprised. Why would that be?

I inquired about the boys, but she seemed not to hear me, although she was staring right at me. How odd for her to act so, and I repeated the question. She heard me this time and told me that Jack and Dick had already departed by car with their father, Pop Turner. Her smile was more than just her ordinary good nature; she was amused. Why, I hadn't a clue. It couldn't have been anything I had said. What could be funny about that?

I told Mrs. Turner I had better hurry along. I didn't let her know, but I was really disappointed that I would now walk about two miles alone to reach the parade area. Mrs. Turner's expression would make the trek with me.

✖

Mrs. Turner had been unprepared for what awaited her when she answered the bell. The uniform I had chosen reached back in time some decade or two. I resembled a WWI doughboy. Long pants and jaunty overseas caps had long ago replaced my ensemble, consisting of riding breeches and knit, knee-length, khaki socks. The crowning glory, literally, was my hat—the "General Pershing," with a flat brim encircling it, appearing as large as an umbrella. It provided enough shade for a whole troop of scouts. I must have looked like a walking manhole cover with a bump on it!

Mrs. Turner's expression had me thinking as I walked down busy Torrance Boulevard. The expressions of passing strollers had a lot in common with hers, and I began to suspect that in my need to look different, to not just be one of the "sheep," I had perhaps gone a bit too far.

As I walked past a store window, I paused to examine my reflection and realized that I looked splendid and ridiculous at the same time. On the one hand, my uniform was new, freshly pressed and fit me perfectly. On the other, I looked like a relic from a time gone by. People would think I had rescued my dad's or granddad's uniform from the cedar chest. My brain had not been receiving enough blood, that was quite obvious.

If it had been 1924 instead of 1944, I surely would have been a poster scout, but this *was* 1944! I looked like a half-wit, I decided. I was certain to get more than polite smiles if I marched in the parade in this get-up, especially from my fellow scouts, so I did some fast thinking and fast moving.

Returning home, I exchanged my breeches for Levi jeans and packed the grand "General Pershing" away. A pity. It really was magnificent, a bit too much so. Tastes had changed.

My mother saw the exchange and asked no questions. She was, I think, quite relieved. Apparently it had been a close call for both of us.

My scout shirt and Levi combination served the purpose just fine. I didn't feel cloned nor did I stick out like a sore thumb. A vivid lesson in compromise, not always easy since intelligent compromise requires considerable blood to the brain.

The down side was that I could hardly have been noticed by any of the girls watching the parade. I wasn't a "faceless clone," but I wasn't a celebrity either. I had strong doubts about the likelihood of ever attaining Eagle. My bet was that I had gone about as far in scouting as I could expect to go. The important thing was what had *almost* happened. My attempt to avoid looking like all the other sheep nearly got me laughed out of the flock.

✖

My grandmother was checking the nests for eggs. It was not good to leave the eggs too long, since hens occasionally got curious and pecked their own eggs. It was like a minor tragedy when we looked, only to find the mess created by a broken egg in the nest, so we checked often. Besides, my grandmother loved to collect eggs. It was rewarding and earthy. I liked it too. I liked everything about my job. Cleaning coops and hutches was the worst of it, but even that was okay. The animals were productive and deserved a clean habitat. My dad told me that if we kept things clean, our animals would be healthy, and once again, he was right. Of all the people we knew doing what we were doing, our animals were the best and the cleanest!

Rabbits were showing up with speckled livers. I didn't know why, and no one else seemed to know either, but people were suspicious and did not want to buy rabbits with this mysterious condition. My dad was convinced he knew and insisted it was for the most basic of all reasons—lack of cleanliness.

There were no sophisticated laboratories around to provide a scientific answer, but we never had a single animal with the condition, and while we held our breath each time a rabbit was butchered, we felt our system was confirmed with each perfect liver we extracted.

Our hens were all kept in coops as well, and as a result, they too were healthy, clean, and more productive than those belonging to our counterpart "mini-farmers." Being successful at something like this was really gratifying and made the whole process a source of pleasure beyond the sales and profits. When people came from some distance for our animals, we were really proud of ourselves.

I longed, however, for the successes in my life to extend a bit further and in a much different direction. Being a successful fledgling farmer was great, but it was one more area of involvement that had no apparent connection with girls. Would I never do anything that took their breath away or even caught their eye?

Frustration must surely be the mother of bad judgment, as I was about to discover. My longings seemed like a gangrenous limb, shriveling and putrefying and hopeless, and so in frustration, I let my emotions overwhelm my common sense. I began to focus on Jean Sparks as the most appropriate solution to my problem; 180 degrees off course.

Did I realize how far ahead of myself this idea propelled me? I had yet to hold hands with a girl, put my arm around one in the darkened theater, even talk to one, to be totally accurate. Yet my mind, freshly marinated with new hormones, convinced me I was on a logical path. Obviously, socializing with older kids, specifically the band members, had given me a poor perspective relative to the proper progression of sexual maturation. It did not occur to me at that moment that much of what I was hearing in these sessions just might not be the total truth either.

✖

Because of my superior, somewhat effeminate handwriting, I had for some time provided my classmate Jack Emerson with a note permitting him to purchase a nudist magazine called *Sunshine and Health*. Jack had an overactive curiosity (didn't we all?) and I saw no harm in it. Besides, I was kind of flattered that my note was honored by the local pharmacist, who was apparently convinced that Mrs. Emerson sent son Jack for the magazine on a monthly basis. He would dutifully wrap it in brown paper for Jack to deliver home.

This gave me an idea. Would such a note permit Jack to purchase rubbers? I asked Jack. He suggested that there should be no problem, my notes were surely convincing enough. In fact, he thought it a grand idea. He would like to own one too, for good reason. Owning a rubber was a status symbol. When placed in one's wallet, it soon formed an unmistakable image of itself on the wallet for all to see, and proud owners made certain as many eyes as possible saw it. Jack was quite excited about the prospect of ownership.

I decided to request Trojans because I wasn't sure if Sheik was spelled with i-e or e-i. They were the only two brands I knew of.

Our partnership remained inactive until we both had saved $2.50. We felt confident that five dollars would buy two rubbers.

The plan was a master stroke of efficiency. Jack obtained not two, but three rubbers (Trojans) and change! In the sack was a note to Mrs. Emerson explaining that the item came in packages of three. I felt mildly guilty about the forgery, since this time I was a beneficiary, but my euphoria overwhelmed my guilt. I was the proud owner of a Trojan rubber. Into my wallet it went. Jean Sparks and I would not be producing a baby!

But I didn't even know Jean Sparks! At least I knew she existed, which was more than she knew about me. This plan was light years from being put into action. Unless I had another stroke of genius, Mr. Trojan was doomed to be only a status symbol, like his two brothers in Jack's wallet. Still, if she let all these other guys do it, wasn't I just as entitled to a share? It was an encouraging point of view. However, would my parents be proud of where my mind was these days? No way! I knew it, but I was becoming a bit irritated that my conscience was always throwing them in the middle of everything I did. My conscience needed to grow up a bit and stop bugging me. Everything produced a gray cloud of guilt hanging over my head.

✠

It was Saturday and Harold came over to see if I wanted to go to the movies. He didn't know what was playing, not that it mattered.

Albert (Boo) and brother Richard were going too. I felt like clearing my head with a bit of light entertainment, so off we went.

Harold was talking about a dirty song Bing Crosby had popularized called "Moonlight Becomes You." I was familiar with the song and puzzled by his opinion, which he explained.

"The part," he said, "where he sings, 'you're all dressed up to go dreaming—mind if I tag along' was clearly a case of Bing inviting himself to bed with Dorothy Lamour," a pornographic suggestion, he thought.

I rolled my eyes. Once again a timely remark that illustrated how hopeless it would be to confide in Harold. Jesus, "Moonlight Becomes You" a dirty song? Maybe he thought "Mary Had a Little Lamb" meant she gave birth to one! I would be glad to get to the theater; our age difference appeared to be widening. Harold seemed to be hanging back, getting every last drop of childhood while I was in free fall toward adulthood. Albert, by comparison, was just going with the flow, letting things happen naturally. Albert's life seemed to have none of the peaks and valleys mine had. I wished I could keep my peaks and, like Albert, avoid the valleys, but I knew it was not to be. I would always be opening some can only to release the entire worm population of planet earth!

What a disaster! I should have checked first. The damned movie was one of those double-feature horror things. A mummy was stalking everyone, and of course, everyone was in the wrong place at the wrong time. The mummy was always inches away from grabbing someone and doing who knows what to them.

Some of the kids laughed at it, but it drove me nuts. I always thought movies were an opportunity to be someone else for a time, so I was usually deeply involved with the characters on the screen. After worrying them through four hours of mummy terror, I was exhausted—a nervous wreck. My fingernails were chewed down to the quick and it had taken a super effort to get them grown out. I was one of those kids that got into that fingernail habit and thought I had it whipped. Now I was back to ground zero. I couldn't pick up a dime if I tried all day.

Lots of kids were with girlfriends. I had real mixed emotions about that. Having a girlfriend would be great, but not at one of these crazy movies. They really made me sweat! Girls liked brave guys; everybody knew that.

None of this mummy stuff affected Harold at all. He was like a table hopper in a restaurant, bouncing around, visiting, oblivious of the disturbance he created. He had a ball, as usual.

Albert and Richard looked a bit green around the gills though. Their reaction was more like mine. They too were glad to get out of that dark theater and into the safety of daylight. Mummies hate daylight.

We had been hoping for the same thing—a Hope and Crosby road picture, or Abbott and Costello, maybe Joe E. Brown, Judy Canova—stuff we could laugh at. We liked comedy and war pictures, especially ones with lots of airplanes, like "A Yank in the RAF" or "Flying Leathernecks." Although I didn't talk about it much, I liked anything with Hedy Lamar. She was so gorgeous. I thought about her a lot, like I did Sheena.

On that subject, the movie had at least given me a chance to exhibit my now embossed wallet at the ticket booth. The reaction was not the desired or anticipated one. The girl in the ticket booth had not appeared impressed or aroused. Her look, to be honest, was more like disgust. But she was not the lusty Jean Sparks, the ultimate target of my treasured Trojan, so I shrugged off the "man hater" in the ticket booth and entered the mummy's tomb.

My investment in the Trojan was just enough to keep me involved in my dirty little scheme. I knew I was in over my head and that complications would make me wish I had used better judgment, but I felt committed. It was like a bargain sale that I couldn't afford but that might never come again. It was by luck that I had learned of Jean Sparks and her sexual generosity. It was my bad luck that I wasn't older. It could be a now-or-never situation, and common sense would have to wait in the wings while I seized the moment. I could sure use a bit more knowledge of the basics, I thought, especially anatomy, and specifically female anatomy.

I had never had the "I'll show you mine if you show me yours" experience, so I was really only "zone"-oriented—the specifics were very hazy. Unfortunately, Jovine never went bottomless, leaving me with mostly guesswork to fall back on. Jack Emerson's *Sunshine and Health* magazine rarely showed a frontal view of the nude body, and then only at a distance and through the bushes. I could only hope the phrase "doin' what comes naturally" could be taken literally and that I would be guided by instinct when the critical time arrived.

My stomach was joining the march of the butterflies again. Why was I doing this?

⊐⊏

Our football team played its games at 3:00 p.m. on Friday after-noons. Our field had no lights, so there were no night games. We played the neighboring towns—most notably, San Pedro, a town with a reputation—very tough. In fact, one of the most dangerous towns in America, according to Ripley.

As the band members prepared for the half-time ceremonies, namely our block letter "T" and morale-infusing fight songs, Sam Hollander, our star halfback, ran for a touchdown right past me as I stood at the sideline. What a thrill!

I thought Sam Hollander looked like Gary Cooper, and he was a senior, which to me was almost like being a movie star. It seemed to me all the female seniors were beautiful and all the male seniors were handsome. They seemed so grown up yet so free of adult hangups. Boy, I wished I was a senior!

We did just great, and the students in the stands were apprecia-tive. They were all charged up with adrenaline already, and we were beneficiaries of the general enthusiastic prevailing attitude. I was re-ally pumped up to be a participant—a giant step above the ordinary spectator level.

The remainder of the game was heart-stopping, settled in the final moments when our fullback, Tom Faren, caught a desperation pass and stumbled into the end zone for the winning score. We all went crazy! It was a major event when Torrance beat San Pedro, and even bigger was the fact that they represented the last major hurdle enroute to the conference championship—the first one ever.

Everybody in the stands spilled onto the field, including the band—and also including Jean Sparks.

The football players knew exactly what to do. They started kissing girls. The idea caught on and spread like a grassfire. Kissing was highly contagious; I could see that.

I thought I was only a spectator, but all of a sudden, I got kissed; my first kiss from a non-relative. I had become the beneficiary of a kissing frenzy. My cape and cap probably duped my kissers into thinking I was older, but it was more likely they didn't even notice whom they were kissing. By the time they realized their mistake, it was too late. They had kissed this child clarinet prodigy. I just remained available, thinking I was really involved and it was fun. I had lots of lipstick on my face, but none of it had belonged to Jean Sparks. In the excitement I had failed to think of her and had missed a possible big-time opportunity.

Besides the kisses, I picked up a significant piece of information. This celebration was to continue at the Civic Auditorium dance tonight. I intended to be there, too. I would have bet that Jean Sparks would be in attendance, and if the kissing frenzy began again, I would be in Jean's proximity. Good plan, I thought. If we were going to mate, we ought to meet first.

The Civic Auditorium Friday night dances had been of no interest to me. I hadn't learned to dance and could not envision myself that close to a girl; besides, most girls I knew were too tall.

The auditorium itself was one of the town landmarks. The Friday dances were essential to eleventh- and twelfth-grade society.

Torrance parents and police were not as supportive. It represented the only real potential for trouble, and during football season, one could almost sense a fuse leading to the auditorium doors. If Torrance won, the losers knew where to look for trouble that night; it had happened all too often. Some very violent scenes had occurred, and tonight had big-time potential, considering that the vanquished was San Pedro.

I was pretty ignorant of all this or I might have given some serious thought to going there. Not only was I not a dancer, but I sure wasn't a fighter either, especially at the level that took place at the Civic. I could get squashed!

It cost a quarter to get in, and they stamped the back of your hand so you could get in and out. Under a special lamp the ticket seller-hand stamper person could see the stamp; otherwise it was invisible. I wondered how they did that.

I felt self-conscious. I was always the smallest, youngest person outside the neighborhood, and I never got used to it. I tried to look taller and older without looking foolish in the process.

There were already quite a few people inside. Nobody was dancing because the band wasn't set up yet. They weren't kissing either. It appeared the kissing frenzy had not survived the trip from the football field to the Civic. My hopes were dashed and my quarter was probably wasted.

The clarinet player was warming up and it was clear he had the same practice ethic as Moe Jarrett. Jesus, he sounded great. Listening to him I felt like giving up, but life without the band was no life at all. Maybe I could find time for a bit more practice. One could practice something besides scales!

It seemed like the auditorium was getting smaller, but it was because people were arriving in large clumps. Then all of a sudden there she was—Jean Sparks. I was getting to the point where I could almost sense her presence before I saw her.

The band began to play "Stardust," and Sam Hollander led Jean onto the dance floor. Jean looked starstruck, while Sam looked as if this happened all the time. I guess it did.

More and more people were dancing, and soon I was one of the few inactive attendees. I restationed myself near the stage and acted like I had come to listen to the band, and, in fact, I was impressed. They were terrific, and it occurred to me that the clarinet player could probably pick any girl in the auditorium and do anything he wanted to. He would be too much competition, even for Sam. I would, as a young clarinet player, become an older clarinet player, and then watch out!

Watching Jean and Sam was not what I had come for, so I decided to return another Friday night when Sam might be busy. I headed for the restroom first.

I almost suffocated! The bathroom was full of smokers. The air was billowing in clouds of thick fumes around the bodies as they moved about in the gloom, sneaking their smokes. Underage people did not smoke in public in the '40s. We called them "weed bangers."

While I was relieving myself, I began to cough, gagging on the thick, fetid air, and I looked down to see I had splashed pee on my trousers. Oh boy, Jean would really be impressed with this. I blotted myself with paper towels, tied my sweater around my waist and went out the door, hoping to exit the auditorium quickly.

The atmosphere was drastically changed, and I'm not referring to the absence of smoke. The large room had become polarized due to a group of very threatening-appearing large people. I could feel the tension, and in an instant the room exploded into shouts, screams. People were dashing every direction. I had no clue where I should be, but I felt far too exposed. I quietly backed toward the wall. The dance floor looked more and more like a battleground to me.

Sam and a few of his teammates were approaching the tough-looking group, and all hell was surely about to break loose. Neither group appeared afraid of the other, which seemed like a mistake to me. I was reminded of western movies where fights broke out in the saloon and involved everybody. I wanted no part of that. I felt about as effective as Gabby Hayes would be in a barroom fight.

I began to inch my way toward the exit, but I did not have a very safe path. The intruders did not want their escape route cut off, and I would not be very smart to get any closer to them. This was a switch; I now tried to look smaller. I was not very comfortable at all; this was more adventurous than I had anticipated, by a bunch.

As if by magic, three cops just seemed to materialize and they did not look understanding at all. I was certain someone was going to get conked with a nightstick, but the intruders, after a long staring session, began to retreat. They still didn't look very intimidated, and I think the cops were very relieved when they left. I know I sure was. They had steamed into harm's way, knowing they would be outnumbered, apparently with no fear for their safety. They were bona fide tough guys. Like my dad, they were "battle ready."

The band came to life with their rendition of "If I Didn't Care," a terrific song popularized by the Ink Spots. The effect was instantaneous. One could feel the tension melt away as couples began to dance once again. Music was a wonderful thing, I thought. In just moments, the mood had gone from open warfare to a state of dreamy reverie.

As I departed, it occurred to me that girls sure seemed happy when they were dancing. That deserved some thought. Sam Hollander danced, I noticed. It was a relief to see Sam dancing with someone else. Jean was talking to a little guy named Kenny Stockwell and looked almost as pleased as if it were Sam. That was really odd. Kenny was a "scrub," a seventh grader.

Kenny was so strange. He was a new scrub, but he knew everyone and everyone treated him in an oddly special way. Juniors and seniors treated him almost like an equal, which was unheard of for a seventh-grader, a scrub. He was very short, not like a midget, muscular, not like a dwarf. He was like a miniature high school senior, so peculiarly grown up while so young and small. If the movie star Victor Mature had been born looking as he did as an adult, at eleven he would have looked like Kenny. It seemed like every girl in school was fascinated by him. Like everyone else, they just couldn't quite believe what they were seeing and couldn't leave him alone. If it were only his physical appearance, the effect would not have been so striking, but he had an equally mature personality. It should have been spooky, but he was so personable that he was magnetic. When he struck up a conversation in his easy way, he made you feel like you were listening to some friend of your parents.

The thing about Kenny that rang my bell was that he obviously knew Jean Sparks. In fact, to see them right now one might suspect they were related. He was chatting with her as easily as if he were Sam Hollander, or John Wayne, for that matter.

Emerging from the ooze of my devious, slimy mind was a plan. Kenny was the entree I needed to complete my sexual liaison with Jean. This was not making me a better person. I would attempt to recruit him, but if I met resistance, I would threaten to beat him up. If threats didn't work, I would probably need to seek a different route. It wouldn't help my popularity if I punched Kenny.

If only I could expect Jean to be so impressed. As soon as I told Kenny I had a rubber, he was mine! Rubbers were magical, I thought. He had to see it, of course, and it took some doing to direct his attention to the mission I was assigning to him. He was hypnotized by the Trojan.

I swore Kenny to secrecy and outlined my plan. He thought it was a wonderful idea. The thought of some sexy dialogue with Jean appealed to him, and as we proceeded, I realized his sexual precocity was running well ahead of mine. It became apparent that he knew more about this mysterious stuff than I did, which was both good and bad. I didn't pump him for information because I was afraid I would lose control. Instead I moved boldly into the specifics.

Kenny would be needed Friday night at the Civic. While I waited, he would advise Jean that I had a rubber and longed to put it to use. That was the plan. Not exactly subtle. If she wasn't motivated by that disclosure, Ken was to tell her that I wanted to perform "sexual intercourse" with her. I stressed the phrase "sexual intercourse" because I felt it was sophisticated and would make a good impression.

Ken did not agree. He suggested a much more direct and vulgar approach, but I stood firm. "Sexual intercourse," I insisted.

Ken was more than supportive; he was openly enthusiastic. He felt it axiomatic that if my plan succeeded, he would almost surely be able to approach Jean on his own behalf. He was displaying genuine lust now, and I really did worry about control. What exactly would Kenny say to Jean, I wondered? He would be talking for someone else and therefore would enjoy a wide degree of immunity in what he said and how he said it. Would he present my proposition or his, I wondered? The torpedo, once fired, was not steerable.

So I rehearsed Kenny two or three times and decided I would have to trust him and my luck. It was not a comfortable view. My luck was not that good, and Kenny seemed a bit unreliable and flighty.

My problems would not end with Jean's acceptance. In fact, they would only get more complicated. "Where" and "when" were only two of the unknowns. "How" would have to be somehow automatic. I sure hoped so, anyway. What a mine field I had gotten myself into.

✂

My personal D-day arrived—Friday, dance night at the Civic. Would Jean Sparks be there? Would Kenny Stockwell show up to carry out his assignment? I wasn't sure what I really wanted, but if she was there and if he appeared, the program would progress as if it had a mind of its own, that I knew. The time bomb was ticking, and I felt like I had no clue how to disarm it at this point.

When I arrived, the large auditorium was filling fast. People who saw each other in school all week saw each other in a completely different context Friday night at the Civic; but I wasn't one of them. I was younger, for one thing, but I saw Jean Sparks in the same context regardless of where we were.

And there she was—my "target for tonight" (the title of a war movie). She was at the far end of the dance floor near the stage, and Sam Hollander was not with her. It was perhaps the first time I had seen her alone. Perfect! Or was it? Butterflies were in migratory flight through my stomach. I felt like I needed some Kaopectate. If Kenny didn't show up, nothing would happen. But before that thought had any chance at reality, Kenny appeared and indicated he was ready to do my bidding. Torpedo tubes ready!

I pulled Kenny aside for one more rehearsal. I didn't really trust him, and once more I insisted on the proper phraseology. He shrugged and agreed. My heart was pounding.

Before leaving, he had a question. "Do you think," he began, "that a rubber can be used more than once?" It didn't take a genius to figure out where his mind was going, so I acted knowledgeable and answered in the negative. He looked a bit disappointed and began the journey across the room to where Jean stood, still alone, thank God! Torpedoes away!

I watched Kenny as if in a hypnotic trance. We both seemed to have a floating quality, and the sounds made by the band and the dancers seemed muted. I could almost hear Kenny's breathing and footsteps.

Kenny seemed to be crossing a vast sea; the dancing people were like rising and falling waves on an endless ocean. Would he ever make it to the far shore? Not before I had a heart attack! My head felt like it was growing and my face was getting hot. I tried to swallow, but my mouth was so dry the process never really got underway. My bathroom sexploits were never traumatic; why had I let things get so complicated? A little guilt was small payment for the gratification one received in the privacy of one's own bathroom. Why hadn't that been enough?

I wished I had tied a string to Kenny so I could have called off the entire thing with a quick tug. It was a great idea, but too late now. Kenny was ashore, standing in front of Jean.

My scrotal sac contracted perceptibly and my head burst into flames. The floor seemed to fall from under me and my legs lengthened to compensate, but they were made of rubber. Was I going to faint?

I watched as Kenny turned and pointed at me. He wasn't supposed to do that. I'll bet he didn't say "sexual intercourse" either. The program was out of control. I could only guess what was going down by now.

Suddenly both Kenny and Jean set sail and began the endless journey to my shore. Oh God, this wasn't how I thought it would happen. Jean was ready for me right now! She was coming to get me and my rubber, Kenny leading the way. I would have to do it tonight, just minutes from now.

I was going to wet my pants, I thought, or the way my stomach felt, something worse! This was disastrous. Jean was ready for me, and I had to go to the bathroom. Surely she would not wait while I excused myself for such a moodbreaking event as bladder or bowel processes to be served. I reached into my pocket and pinched off my penis, which seemed to have shrunk just when it was going to need size.

They were almost here. Could Jean see what my hand was doing? My mind projected an image of my penis compared to Sam Hollander's. Oh God, what have I done? If Jean saw my pitiful member, the whole world would know. It would be too good to keep to herself, and I would be the main subject among male band members Monday.

And then she stood before me, smiling down at me. It hadn't occurred to me that she was so much taller than I, and it made me really uncomfortable. Kenny's presence helped. He was much shorter yet and made me feel a bit taller anyway. I tried to be taller yet; not easy to do.

Jean said, "Hi, LeRoy" in a coquettish way that almost took my breath away. I had hoped that at this moment I would be so cool, so controlled that any girl would be impressed with my uncharacteristic maturity. I wanted to act like Clark Gable. Women couldn't resist him, he was so cool. Even Kenny was cooler than I!

As I was trying to look older and taller, maintaining just the right pressure on my penis to stem the flow of urine my bladder was insisting should be released, I tried to focus some concentration on what Jean was saying to me.

The sound of Jean's voice seemed far off as I stared at her mouth, trying to keep from soaking my clothes with sweat or urine. Other voices, as well as the band sounds, again seemed to fade further and further into the background. We were almost alone, surrounded by all these nameless, faceless, other-dimensional people. Jean's voice seemed like it was coming from the bottom of a well.

What Jean said was that I was "still a bit too young and little," although she thought I was "really cute." I sensed a "no" and struggled to project a cavalier attitude.

My mind wasn't remotely on sex. Somehow the thought had just evaporated when Jean arrived before me, and soon I was once again tumbling in the interior of a monstrous wave, so overpowered that I couldn't even make the most feeble attempt to control myself, headed straight down to the sandy bottom.

"I have a favor to ask, LeRoy," she said. "Kenny says you have a Trojan, and I would really like you to loan it to Sam Hollander. Would you do that for me? It would be so sweet of you."

I found myself reaching for my wallet, and before I realized it, I had delivered up my most prized and impressive possession—and just as suddenly, Jean was gone, lost in the sea from which she had come—on her way to a secret place with Sam Hollander, who would be using my rubber. A loan, did she say? A loan? Did that mean Sam would be returning it, somewhat tainted, to say the least? Or would he be presenting me with a new one, purchased specifically to repay me for my generosity? Perhaps two, as a gesture of gratitude for making this a special and unexpected night of pleasure? Did she even say "Thank you"?

Stripped of my fantasy night of bliss as well as my prized rubber, I decided to head home. The longer I hung around the Civic, the more foreign and uncomfortable it seemed. I relieved myself first.

What had gotten into me, anyway, I wondered as I walked the two miles home? I had chosen to leave an uncomplicated and comfortable stage of life and propel myself into the turbulence of a place where I was, as yet, unprepared to function. I felt mild humiliation, but the main emotion was foolishness. I felt like an experienced body surfer who had deliberately caught a pounder. Dumb! But I had survived, and it was over. Relief was beginning to transcend foolishness and stupidity.

I worried that the story would circulate and the other kids would make me feel like an idiot, but I had been holding the tail of a tiger since my brain had soaked up hormones like a glazed donut—I was beginning to feel like a lucky survivor.

I had been, I decided, not unfortunate, but very lucky indeed. Sam Hollander was where he belonged, and I was where I belonged. Let him keep the rubber. I wouldn't need it or any other for a long time. Pretty soon I intended to ask Yvonne Thomas to go to the movies, even if older guys were interested in her. Maybe we would hold hands. That would be wonderful, I thought. I made a resolution to grow up more gradually. Perhaps it would be better to hang back a bit and let someone else get caught in the pounders. I would be more careful in the future, on the lookout for life's dirty tricks and trap doors.

✠

My wallet carried the ghost image of the missing condom. All during its existence, I had hidden it from my parents and Grandma Ellen, and there had been some close calls. I needed a new wallet. I took the pictures out of the celluloid protectors and "lost" the wallet where it would never be found, and went to sleep that night as soon as my head hit the pillow. Jean Sparks was now a subject in my past.

✖

My fiasco with Jean Sparks put me in a mood to do some evaluating—to mentally compile one of those "pros and cons of life" lists.

It was not a fair contest since the process began, for some reason, over one of Anna's heavenly malts. Negatives were hard to focus on with such nectar in one's mouth. Psychiatrists take note: great chocolate malts cure depression.

But malt or no malt, things were really pretty darned good in my life, I thought. I had become a teenager. There had been a time I never thought age thirteen would arrive. And with it, at last, the appearance of body hair, which made gym class a place to hone my budding athletic skills without feeling so self-conscious. I loved sports more every day.

I was an eighth-grader now, not a lowly scrub. I had just a little status anyway, no longer at the bottom rung. I was feeling better and better about myself.

I didn't worry about swats anymore; I realized I was not really the target the swatters sought. I was a bit independent, but not rebellious. With a bit of time, my forgotten locker location and combination nightmares would surely begin to fall away.

Despite the absence of my two sweet Japanese tutors, I was doing okay in my studies, which meant things were okay at home, too.

The war was reaching a crescendo; a major Allied invasion was anticipated at any time. Because there was still a war, I still had my great job and income! Our mini-farm was a financial bonanza for me.

I lived only a short five miles from the beach and the salty surf that almost seemed to course through my veins. Surfing, sports, and band—a triumvirate of pleasures too sweet to believe. Life was good!

With difficulty I struggled to conjure up the negatives, but I had to admit my bathroom fantasies and activities continued to torture me. Control would wax and wane, my resolve would fall away, and I thought I was a vile person at times. My parents would not like me if they knew about all this.

And was it as unhealthy as I had heard? I had to stop so the guilt would go away. I would try harder, but I wouldn't soon go looking for a genuine female partner. No thanks, not again! It was not likely anyway; girls just kind of ignored us like we were invisible. Sports were better anyway, was my opinion. I meant to keep the word "score" reserved for football and baseball. Was there a chance this mysterious girl business would ultimately begin to solve itself? Since clues were so scarce, perhaps, just perhaps, that was the system.

Because I had money to spend—my "rancher's" wages—I tried to insist on supporting my own soda fountain habit, but Anna usually—not always—refused my payment.

Howdy's and the Pacific Lane society.... I had forgotten to include them in the list of positives. My cup runneth over! It and they were always there, like a haystack that would break my various falls in the thin, dangerous atmosphere outside the neighborhood.

We lived two lives, the Pacific Laners. At school we had formed friendships outside the loop, but we all knew the haystack was there and would embrace us when it was needed. We couldn't solve each other's problems, as a rule. We were rarely addressing the same problem at the same time, and we lacked the wisdom anyway. But we could escape for brief periods and breathe, and regain some strength and reenter the arena, refreshed and fortified. We were a lucky—no, a blessed—bunch of kids.

As usual, there was a generous glob of ice cream at the bottom of my malt glass. It kind of represented the wonderful kid life I had going for me. I was savoring both.

I thanked Anna, waved at a few kids, and set out for home and my chickens and rabbits. I walked down Portola Street, past Freda and Irma's house, Bonnie and Verdell Galloway's house, Glen Mitchell's house, Couburn's tiny market, and I was home. I knew every crack in the sidewalk like it was part of my house, and in fact, it was. The invisible walls of the neighborhood embraced us all and created a kinship, perhaps not so thick as blood, but a lot thicker than water. Being there introduced and underscored the phenomenon of friendship and the security of belonging. It always seemed to me that Pacific Lane was in great measure responsible for starting us in the right direction—happier people because, by some great good fortune, we had been kids there and then.

EPILOGUE

Like any story, as this one ends another begins, and the fear is that I have memorialized the trivial and failed to recognize the significant.

The end of the war was so remarkable that I can't stop short of it. It was, arguably, the most significant set of events in world history.

Wars, like people, have much in common, while at the same time they differ vastly; each one leaves a unique print as it arrives and departs.

World War II was a war the American people didn't want...until Japan's sneak attack. Probably never before and never again will the American people be so nearly unanimous in their pro-war resolve.

Not only the kids but everyone fantasized about our scientists developing a "secret weapon." How could we know that our dream would come true, and that the weapon would be too good?

Controversy will continue forever about the use of the atomic bomb, but it is only a fool's exercise; once the genie is out of the bottle, he can't be returned. A war-ending weapon can't be hidden or ignored.

The enemy had been cruel, as enemies always are, and mercy was in very short supply—perhaps nonexistent. The Japanese and Germans were commonly perceived as a two-headed monster, and horrendous discoveries of German atrocities had been transferred to the still-living head—Japan. Almost to a person, we celebrated our grand victory; the A-bomb was our hero.

As to the events of this book, they are factual, or very close to it. I admit that memory is not exact after half a century, but what I wrote is how I remember it.

Pacific Lane itself requires no remembering—it remains nearly unchanged from the first day I saw it in July of 1939. The Nash Ambassador is missing, of course, but the tiny houses remain as if time has stood still. Standing there, I can almost hear the voices of my childhood friends; I can picture their faces clearly. Where has the time gone?

The people are real, some names are changed, but all these wonderful characters will recognize themselves should they ever read my words.

There were a lot more kids I failed to include, most notably Reuben Zamora and Roy Aguilar—special friends who will be featured prominently if I ever find the energy to continue this and include my early teens.

Since I wrote mainly about my struggles and ordeals, I hope I didn't leave the wrong impression. It was a grand experience to grow up in Torrance in the 1940s, and I'm sure many kids from other neighborhoods can match my grand experiences, event for event.

The Pacific Lane parents deserve special consideration. They were all wonderful, adding to the cohesiveness of the neighborhood.

In spite of the surprise surgical extra during my tonsillectomy, my parents were wonderful, and there was never a moment I could have questioned their love for me. I have tried to assure my mother she need suffer no guilt; I consider it an amusing, not a traumatic, event. It's okay, Mom, honest.

My final word on the events herein....

If anyone who might read this knows Chizuko or Sakio, I need to know if they made it through those years okay, and I pray they managed to find some happiness when the craziness of their "relocation" was over. I'm sorry about the airplane incident, girls.